NONPROFIT LIFECYCLES

Stage-based Wisdom for Nonprofit Capacity

SECOND EDITION

By Susan Kenny Stevens, Ph.D.

With a Foreword by
Paul C. Light

Winner of the Alliance for Nonprofit Management's
Terry McAdam Book Award for most valuable nonprofit
book published in 2002.

Publisher: Stagewise Enterprises, Inc.
215 Otis Avenue; Suite B
St. Paul, MN 55104

Design and production: Wallinga Design, Minneapolis, MN
Editor: White Fence Communications, Minneapolis, MN

Printed in the United States of America

Library of Congress Cataloguing Publication Data
Stevens, Susan Kenny.
Nonprofit Lifecycles: Stage-based Wisdom for Nonprofit Capacity
ISBN 0-9717305-0-4

First edition, March 2002
Second edition, September 2008

Dedication

To my Stevens Group and LarsonAllen co-workers
who were early adopters of the concepts in this book,
and to the hundreds of lifecycle converts
who will carry this work forward in the years ahead.
I am in your debt.

In theory,
there is no difference
between theory and practice.
But in practice there is.

Jan L. A. Van de Snepscheut

Other Books by this Author

Growing Up Nonprofit™

Cashing In
A Nonprofit's Introduction to Borrowing Money

Keeping the Books

All The Way to the Bank
Smart Money Management for Tomorrow's Nonprofit

Investing In Capacity

Budgeting Your Way to Financial Stability

The Warhol Initiative
Capacity-building for the Visual Arts

TABLE OF CONTENTS

FOREWORD

We meet them where they are. The phrase comes as close to a core commandment of capacity building as the nonprofit sector gets. Capacity builders and funders have long believed that clients and grantees should decide for themselves how to increase their own effectiveness. That is in part because capacity builders are appropriately humble about the precision of their own instruments, and in part because clients are rightly skeptical about the pay-offs of reform.

Unfortunately, "meeting nonprofits where they are" often gets translated into "meeting nonprofits wherever they happen to be." Lacking a basic theory about what might work at any given point in an organization's life span, capacity builders have had little choice but to offer menus of possible interventions from which their clients or grantees can pick and choose regardless of the potential for success, including the latest fads coming out of the governmental and private sectors.

Nothing could be more unhelpful as the nonprofit sector confronts the call to higher performance. Although some interventions work, whether because of good luck or random probability, the sector wastes too much of its precious time and energy on interventions that come too early or late in an organization's life. The result is needless motion, wasted effort, ongoing disappointment, and a lingering sense that the nonprofit sector just cannot quite get its act together when it comes to organizational effectiveness.

Luckily, there is an alternative in Susan Steven's work on the stages of nonprofit life. Building on twenty years of active consulting and her wonderful, earlier work, *Growing Up Nonprofit™*, Susan rightly believes that organizations go through different stages of life, moving from the idea stage to start-up, growth, maturity, decline, turnaround, and, where appropriate, termination.

Some interventions will help an organization move from start-up to growth, but be virtually useless in stemming decline or sparking a turnaround. Other interventions are "age-appropriate" for the idea stage, but hopelessly unhelpful at termination. Finally, someone has given real traction to the phrase "meeting organizations where they are." For Susan, lifecycle management is the central challenge for nonprofit organizations. It most certainly should be part of every curriculum for training nonprofit leaders.

I first came upon Susan's work in the early 1990s while doing my own research on sustaining innovation in a sample of Minnesota nonprofits. Although she had touched many of the exemplary organizations I was studying through her own consulting practice, Susan's greater contribution to sustaining innovation was in helping nonprofits understand the natural, even inexorable aging process that affects all human organizations, be they governmental, private, or nonprofit.

The fact that all organizations age does not mean that the process is similar across sectoral boundaries, however. We have long known that government agencies are nearly immortal, for example, and that small businesses suffer a remarkably high failure rate in the first year of existence. Susan does not claim, therefore, that her model holds for all organizations in all sectors. Rather, she bounds her work with clear examples that suggest its enormous potential for helping nonprofit capacity builders target their work more effectively.

Unlike those who study change without ever engaging it, Susan's work is designed to help nonprofits diagnose their own place on the lifecycle, and take action to avoid the pitfalls of youth, middle-age, and senescence. If not quite a fountain of youth, *NONPROFIT LIFECYCLES* is most certainly a fountain of ideas for making choices about how to sustain effectiveness at different stages of the lifecycle. As such, it is the right book at the right time, and essential reading for anyone who truly wishes to meet nonprofits where they are.

Paul C. Light
Washington, DC

INTRODUCTION

This is the book I have always wanted to write. It presents the lifecycle approach to nonprofit capacity that has been the cornerstone of my work over the past three decades as an organizational consultant to nonprofits and foundations.

This book began as the monograph, *Growing Up Nonprofit* ™, written first in 1988 and reprinted three times since. Originally developed for non-profit managers and their board members, *Growing Up Nonprofit* ™ introduced the lifecycle tasks, challenges, and inevitable growing pains that nonprofits could expect to encounter and hope to master on the road to institutional maturity.

Since drafting the original monograph, my colleagues and I have used the lifecycle model contained in *Growing Up Nonprofit* ™ to diagnose and explain organizational capacity and behavior to more than ten thousand nonprofit managers and foundation officers through individual consulta-tions and skill-building seminars.

Now, as the importance of organizational capacity to nonprofit effec-tiveness has so prominently hit center stage, there seems no better time than the present to showcase lifecycle theory and its stage-based application to nonprofit capacity. And the time is indeed right.

Throughout the country, foundations, nonprofit board members, and managers are realizing that, in the long run, nonprofits' ability to deliver programs and services is only as good as their overall institutional health, durability, and competence.

Yet, as a concept, *capacity* is still too broad to be of practical help to nonprofits or their funders.

> Capacity building is a popular term these days ~ too pop-ular and expansive a term, in fact, to mean much to individuals making specific decisions about their programs and grant strategies. As a result, everyone, from practi-tioners to foundation CEOs, is calling for increased attention to the capacity building needs of nonprofit orga-nizations. So far, however, the rhetoric is ahead of the work. (Penelope McPhee and John Bare, *Capacity Building in Nonprofit Organizations*, 2001[i])

3

And so, to a field abuzz with concepts such as *capacity-building, venture philanthropy, innovation, high performance* and *best practice,* this book, *NONPROFIT LIFECYCLES,* weighs in with a developmental perspective on nonprofit capacity and its relationship to increased performance.

The lifecycle approach to organizational growth and maturation is grounded in at least a century of developmental and organizational theory. It is an eminently practical model that takes a holistic view of the entire organization and captures the stage-related growing pains that generally accompany each phase of development. The more accurate the diagnosis of an organization's stage, the better managers can manage, and funders can target capacity-related services that make a difference.

The beauty of the lifecycle application to nonprofit capacity is that it works! In fact, it makes so much sense, and is so intuitively logical, that it is easy to ignore how deeply profound and imperative are its lessons and implications.

The lifecycle approach to nonprofit capacity unbundles all-purpose definitions of capacity into a set of discrete stages defined by the competencies and performance measurements associated with each stage.

The lifecycle model uses twin concepts of *diagnosis* and *starting point* to determine organizational capacity. Diagnosis, although medically-associated, is a judgement-neutral term that pinpoints an organization's starting capacity, then designs an appropriate game plan for strengthening the current position or progressing positively to the next developmental stage.

Besides describing typical stage patterns, lifecycle theory can be used to diagnose abnormal patterns of development too ~ founders who don't adapt to the changing management requirements of their organizations, board members with mature expectations out of sync with the start-up agency's reality, and once venerable organizations whose programs have ceased to be relevant.

This book is organized into three sections. The first section presents the rationale for a lifecycle/stage-based approach to nonprofit capacity and a full description of the seven stages of the lifecycle model. You'll also find a *Nonprofit Lifecycles Reference Guide* that presents the diagnostic characteristics and performance indicators of capacity at each of the seven stages. This *Reference Guide* (found in Chapter 4) can be used by nonprofits and funders alike to diagnose starting capacity, assess targeted capacity improvements consistent with the stage, and set realistic performance expectations once the capacity improvement has been accomplished.

Section Two is written especially for nonprofit managers and board members. It contains a discussion of some of the most common and diffi-

The lifecycle approach to nonprofit capacity unbundles all-purpose definitions of capacity into a set of discrete stages defined by the competencies and performance measurements associated with each stage.

cult critical junctures that frequently lead organizations to stall in their development. These challenges include founder transitions, second stage management, developing board ownership, and effecting a nonprofit turnaround. Each chapter in this section contains a brief discussion of the topic and then a prototypical case example, highly reflective of the complex dynamics that are part and parcel of nonprofit management and governance at various stages of life. Each case guides the nonprofit reader on how to use the lifecycle model as an organizational assessment tool. This section also includes a discussion of lifecycle "fit," since by temperament, some of us are more predisposed to working in one lifecycle stage than another.

Section Three discusses how foundations can use the lifecycle approach to create capacity-building programs, make capacity-related grants, and develop targeted capacity interventions. Chapter 10 contains several examples of foundations already using the lifecycle model as the basis for designing or evaluating their capacity-building initiatives. Chapter 11 presents a thorough discussion of the relationship between capacity-building and organizational change, highlighting the key concepts necessary to attain sustainable organizational change and transformation.

There is new and updated information throughout this second edition of *NONPROFIT LIFECYCLES;* but those familiar with the first edition published in 2002 will note substantial content additions to three chapters in particular: *Chapter 6: The Founder's Lifecycle; Chapter 8: Building Your Bench; and Chapter 10: Value-Added Investing.* The content changes and additions to these chapters are a product of my ongoing experience and scholarship in these particular subjects and my eagerness to share this continued interest with the reader.

How I Came to Lifecycle Theory

I came to lifecycle theory early in my second career as a nonprofit management consultant. I'd spent the first fifteen years of my career as a social worker and family counselor specializing in adolescent development. In these roles, I frequently had to make judgements that distinguished normal adolescent growing pains from more serious problematic behaviors. Complex as the many issues I encountered were, they all related to a single developmental period, adolescence. Armed with a fairly good understanding of the predictable characteristics and challenges of this one discrete stage, I was able to diagnose and analyze the behavioral problems presented by my adolescent clients based on a set of commonly held norms.

As I began my consulting business, The Stevens Group, I quickly realized that I was now without such norms. The few management books I

> The beauty of the lifecycle application to nonprofit capacity is that it works! In fact, it makes so much sense, and is so intuitively logical, that it is easy to ignore how deeply profound and imperative are its lessons and implications.

found in libraries or bookstores were geared mainly to Fortune 500 companies or to the owners of small businesses. As nonprofit management books later became more readily available, their advice and protocols still seemed better suited to mature organizations with governing boards, management depth, discretionary resources, and procedural capabilities, than the small and mid-sized clients I was consulting with at the time.

I remember vividly the circumstances that led me to develop the lifecycle approach to nonprofit capacity. A consultant new to our firm asked me to explain why the strategic planning processes we were designing for two social service clients were so dissimilar, despite undeniable similarities of the organizations' missions, clients, and even programming.

My answer was simple. "They're starting from different places."

Although both agencies had provided vital human services to otherwise underserved neighborhoods for the past twenty years, their day-to-day functioning was as different as night and day. Each operated with a budget in the million-dollar range. Yet one of the groups had become a mature, self-directed community resource with professional management, a policy-making board, and sound financial practices. The other had suffered through countless changes in leadership on both the staff and board level, and, for whatever reason, had never taken the necessary steps to move beyond a crisis mode of management. Consequently, although each needed a strategic plan, our approach to one organization had to be much more fundamental than the other. They were starting from different places. If our approach didn't acknowledge that, our plan would be ultimately unsuccessful.

It was in trying to explain the necessity for these vastly differing approaches to the same process that I drew out a bell curve with seven stages of organizational development: *Idea, Start-up, Growth, Maturity, Decline, Turnaround, and Terminal.*

Figure 1: Nonprofit Lifecycle Stages

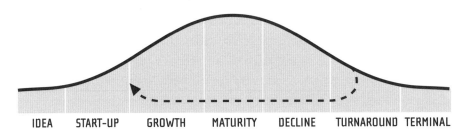

| IDEA | START-UP | GROWTH | MATURITY | DECLINE | TURNAROUND | TERMINAL |

Later in this book you'll see I have since added a further dimension to two of the more complex stages, *growth* and *decline*. But by and large, the lifecycle model I drew out that day has served as the diagnostic framework for assessing the starting capacity point for each of our clients since the late 1980s.

The lifecycle framework has also served as a backdrop for the dozens of capacity programs my Stevens Group and LarsonAllen colleagues developed, managed or evaluated for the Ford Foundation's Working Capital Fund, the Andrew W. Mellon Foundation's Small Press Program, the Geraldine R. Dodge Foundation's Institute for the Advancement of the Arts, the Cleveland Foundation's BASICS Program, the Warhol Initiative, Rose Community Foundation's "BOOST" Program, the Gifford Foundation's ADVANS Program, and many others. Similarly other consultants have adapted our framework and materials to describe the lifecycle development of community foundations, regional grantmaker organizations, and other nonprofit sub-sectors.

Like any book, *NONPROFIT LIFECYCLES* stands on the shoulders of the experience, wisdom, and insights of many others. In fact, every descriptive characteristic and performance indicator contained in this book is a testament to the nonprofits I've met through the years who have tackled head-on the challenges of their particular lifecycle stage and strengthened their overall capacity, or progressed to the next level.

There are three colleagues without whose early support and encouragement this book would have never come to be. Twenty years ago, Elizabeth Schott and Barrie Pribyl gave me the necessary moral and financial support to put the first lifecycle monograph and seminar materials into print. Since then, Anne Howden and my colleagues at LarsonAllen have helped me preach the lifecycle gospel in seminars throughout the country. And now, from southern California to upstate New York, a host of foundations and consultants use "lifecycles" as the organizing principle for their capacity work.

Since writing the first edition of this book, I have made a lifecycle transition of my own ~ from full-throttle to semi-retired. As I leave my career-building years to pursue my own "second act," I am reminded of the many rewards that have accompanied my past three decades as a strategic adviser to so many nonprofits and foundations. By far my greatest satisfactions have come from the capacity-building work I have done using the lifecycles approach outlined in this book. I am equally happy that this approach has now found its way into the vocabulary and repertoire of hundreds of foundations, nonprofits, consultants and academic institutions. Thank you for carrying my work forward and making it your own.

Permission to Skip Ahead

Finally, valued reader, although I have gone to some lengths in the first two chapters to construct the theoretical foundation for a lifecycle approach to capacity, for those of you who want to delve right into lifecycle diagnostics, the heart of this book, I encourage you to head straight to Chapters 3 and 4. There you'll find complete descriptions of each of the seven lifecycle stages, and a multi-part *Nonprofit Lifecycles Reference Guide* of the predictable characteristics and performance outcomes that accompany each lifecycle stage.

Skim over the first two chapters without guilt. The theory, important as it is, will still be there, as it has been for the better part of the last century, when you come back to read it later.

Part One: NONPROFIT CAPACITY

1

CAPACITY COUNTS

Let's start with an assumption, a belief, if you will, that a nonprofit organization is more likely to reach its programmatic goals if it is well managed.

Barbara Kibbe

Of all the innovative practices I've witnessed through the years, potentially the most powerful is the rapidly-spreading acknowledgement among nonprofits and funders that organizational capacity does indeed matter. And it's about time!

For centuries, groups of committed individuals have responded to society's service and cultural gaps by forming charitable organizations. Whether dedicated to healthcare, advocacy, human services, education, arts, or community development, the founders of these nonprofits shared a common trait: they saw a societal void and they filled it. Despite long hours and low pay, without aspirations of wealth or profit, nonprofits focus instead on improving the lives of individuals and communities and, for that, the Internal Revenue Service confers tax-exempt status.

When we turned the calendar to the twenty-first century, there were more than one million nonprofit organizations in the United States alone. Employing over ten million people[ii] and aided by millions of volunteers who serve without pay in governance and service roles, these nonprofits are supported annually by nearly $30 billion in philanthropic support.[iii]

By all accounts the nonprofit sector is growing, continuing to fill greater societal voids while operating in an increasingly competitive resource environment. The importance of nonprofits to society makes an even stronger argument for attending to the organizational as well as programmatic competencies of the sector.

For grantmakers, nonprofit board members, and even individual donors, it may once have been enough to support nonprofits because of an

> If our society does indeed depend on nonprofit organizations for essential service delivery, then these organizations must have the wherewithal to become strong, capable, durable institutions.

11

implicit, albeit unsubstantiated, belief that "they do good work." But with society's current focus on effectiveness and accountability, nonprofits have come under increased scrutiny to demonstrate outcomes, performance, and results.

While foundations, academics and practitioners scurry to articulate, conceptualize, define, and measure what makes nonprofit organizations successful, one thing is becoming more readily understood: *nonprofits cannot achieve or sustain program success without overall organizational competence.* This recognition has led to the creation of several philanthropic capacity-building initiatives, as well as countless self-generated nonprofit capacity improvements, several of which are spotlighted throughout this book.

In addition to their own initiatives, foundation officers have developed collaborative networks with other funders interested in nonprofit capacity, performance, and effectiveness. One group in particular, Grantmakers for Effective Organizations, has mobilized several hundred foundation members in an effort to further explore what makes for effective nonprofit organizations, and by inference, for effective grantmaking. Clearly, nonprofit capacity, performance, and effectiveness are hot topics.

But perhaps the real upshot of the capacity movement lies in the *expectation* it has generated among forward-thinking foundations and nonprofits about the importance of achieving internal capacity and producing results. And human motivation theories, as well as theories of organizational change, consistently support what we know intuitively: *higher expectations generally produce higher results.* Raise the bar, and performance will follow. With this new mindset, nonprofit capacity becomes an expectation rather than a luxury.

Defining Capacity

The somewhat illusory definition of capacity has created a semantic blur around three organizational concepts: *capacity, performance,* and *effectiveness.* Although frequently used synonymously, these are actually three separate and distinct concepts, each important in its own way.

Briefly described, *capacity* is another word for organizational capability and competence. *Performance* is the achievement of measurable goals or objectives. And though there is no universal agreement on the subject, I think of *effectiveness* as an organization's ability to consistently perform in a manner by which its actions have the desired impact on constituents and society.

> Foundations' embrace of organizational capacity and effectiveness reflects the irrefutable fact that, like any other business, nonprofits cannot fully accomplish their programs or mission without overall institutional durability, health, and competence.

These three concepts, *capacity, performance,* and *effectiveness* form a continuum of organizational success with capacity as the means, performance the measurement, and effectiveness as the ultimate goal.

Figure 2: Continuum of Organizational Success

The lifecycle approach presented in this book relates primarily to the concept of capacity and performance. It assumes that the organizational competencies required at each stage may look quite different from one stage to another. What is high-performing behavior in the start-up years would be generally considered underachievement for mature organizations. The management and board characteristics necessary to lead a turnaround would be out of place in a growing organization.

Rather than all-purpose capacity definitions that assume a similar set of expectations and protocols most suitable to mature organizations (a policy-making board, strategic plans, or operating reserve funds), the lifecycle definition of capacity assumes that organizational competence will look different at various stages of the nonprofit development cycle.[iv]

FIVE LIFECYCLE CAPACITY BUILDERS

- Programs
- Management
- Governance
- Financial resources
- Systems

Capacity Builders

In conjunction with *stage theory* that provides the anchor framework for the lifecycle approach to nonprofit capacity, there are at least five *capacity builders* that define the competency framework for each lifecycle stage.

Although universally applicable to each stage, these five capacity builders ~ programs, management, governance, financial resources, and systems ~ will look quite different from stage to stage. The management capabilities required for the *start-up stage* of operation will be quite different from what is required to successfully manage a *mature* organization. Similarly, one could reasonably expect the administrative systems of a *mature* organization to be more streamlined and efficient than those of an organization in an earlier phase of life.

A quick visual might be in order here. Picture for a minute a table upon which you're about to place a breath-taking floral arrangement in a treasured glass vase. As you set the arrangement on the table, you realize that one (or more) of the table's legs is wobbly. Worse yet, one of the legs appears to be shorter than the others. Clearly the fragility of this table puts your prized vase and its contents in jeopardy.

You have many decisions available: prop up the table legs(s) and hope for the best; find another table with more solid legs; or get out the hammer, nails, and glue, and invest the time and energy to strengthen the legs once and for all. But one thing is clear. Unless you attend to the table's wobbly, uneven legs, you can prop the table up all you want, but your eyes will always be diverted away from the vase, and instead, to the leg(s) you are most worried about.

So, too, for nonprofits who've set their treasured mission and programs on wobbly legs. All energy becomes diverted to propping up the weak leg, and thus away from their primary reason to be.

Like the program table analogy, nonprofit capacity demands an equally balanced support system of management, governance, financial resources, and systems to support its mission and programs and in keeping with community need.

Figure 3: Nonprofit Capacity ~ "Table Legs" Supporting Mission and Programs

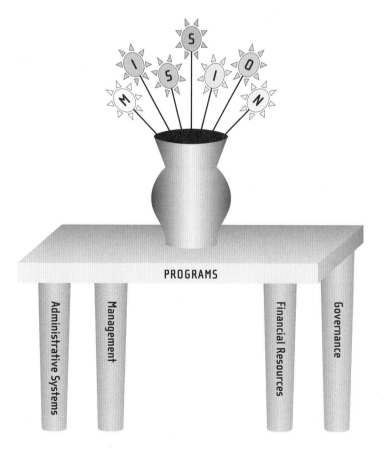

> Nonprofit capacity, from a lifecycle perspective, can be defined as an organization's ability to achieve balance or complete alignment between its programs, management, governance, financial, and other structural requirements at each stage of life.

So, from a lifecycle perspective, nonprofit capacity can be defined as *an organization's ability to achieve balance or complete alignment among its programs, management, governance, financial, and other structural requirements at each stage of life.*

Chapter 4 presents a complete *Nonprofit Lifecycles Reference Guide* of stage-based capacity building requirements ~ programs, management, governance, financial resources and systems ~ as well as a full discussion of the damaging effects to capacity when any of these elements is out of alignment with the overall lifecycle stage.

Capacity Costs

The push to get a better grip on grant results led some foundations in the 1990s to move away from operating support grantmaking and, instead, to embrace a program-grant focus. This shift did what it was intended to do. It helped nonprofits become more concerned about accountability and program outcomes, and it gave funders a much simpler measurement for tracking their own grant results. It's natural to want to direct as much money toward programming as possible. But the arbitrary separation of program from infrastructure has led to the precarious state in which many nonprofits now find themselves, with mission and programs set on a table too wobbly to provide adequate support.

I have written elsewhere on the incapacitating qualities of program-only funding.[v] The gist of these writings is this: program grants may get a job done and accounted for, but they add no value to an organization's capacity.

Several other authors, too, have written convincingly on the "culture of inadequacy,"[vi] the "deadweight" presumption of overhead,[vii] and general funder wariness of administrative costs.[viii] Indeed, led by the admonitions of the Internal Revenue Service and various charity watchdog groups to minimize funds for administrative costs, many nonprofits and foundations have shied away from investing in anything that might look like "overhead." But it is precisely those things we consider overhead ~ a bookkeeper's salary, an audit, administrative help ~ that improve the infrastructural capabilities of an organization to perform.

Although these types of admonitions prepare us intellectually to accept the importance of organizational capacity to nonprofit performance, many have not quite faced the accompanying fact that capacity doesn't come cheap. If capacity does indeed matter, then we must be prepared to pay for it.

The accounting industry has traditionally used the term "capacity costs" to describe, in utilization terms, the financial requirements of achieving organizational efficiency. Transposing this concept to nonprofits,

All too many nonprofits focus on creating new programs and keeping administrative costs low instead of building the organizational capacity necessary to achieve their aspirations effectively and efficiently. This is not surprising, given that donors and funders have traditionally been more interested in supporting an exciting new idea than in building an organization that can effectively carry out that idea. This must change; both nonprofit managers and those that fund them must recognize that excellence in programmatic innovation and implementation are insufficient for nonprofits to achieve lasting results. Great programs need great organizations behind them. (*Effective Capacity Building in Nonprofit Organizations.* Venture Philanthropy Partners, 2001[ix]) *capacity costs are the costs necessary to achieve organizational competence.*

In hindsight, many funders see that the prior practice of supporting programmatic interests only, although easier to measure in terms of outcomes, may have been counterproductive to the achievement of organizational capacity.

Now, as we attempt to make up for lost time and establish an expectational culture of capacity, the price tag could be quite daunting. All the more reason to target investments of time, money, and materials in a manner that is strategically consistent with the lifecycle needs of the organization.

2

STAGE-BASED APPROACH TO NONPROFIT CAPACITY

I think of myself as a bus driver. My job is to pick people up on the corner where they stand and take them where they need to go.

Br. Michael McEnery, F.S.C.

Baby-boomers. The terrible-twos. Adolescence. Mid-life crisis. These are terms we use everyday to describe, and in effect, to codify, distinct periods of human development and the predictable behavioral expectations associated with each. These terms also illustrate *stage theory,* a set of assumptions that (human) development is marked by critical junctures and milestones that result in qualitative changes in capabilities and characteristic behaviors at each phase of life.

Developmental Stage Theory

For more than a century, psychologists have employed stage theory to diagnose and compare individual behaviors against normative ("normal") developmental patterns.

Erik Erikson was among the first to believe that human development occurs in a series of stages. Erikson proposed that development is an eight-stage process, beginning with infancy and ending with old age. He named each of these stages for a particular challenge or *psychosocial crisis* (a combination of internal and external factors) that every individual must resolve to be able to move on to the next stage.

Erikson believed that successful mastery of the psychosocial crisis at a particular stage results in a personality strength or virtue that helps individuals meet future developmental challenges. Furthermore, Erikson believed these psychosocial conflicts are never fully resolved, and despite what progress individuals might achieve in moving through the challenges

Stage theory is a set of assumptions that (human) development is marked by critical junctures and milestones that result in qualitative changes in capabilities and characteristic behaviors at each phase of life.

ERIK ERIKSON'S PSYCHOSOCIAL STAGES OF DEVELOPMENT

Stage One – *Trust* versus *mistrust*. The proper balance between trust and mistrust in infancy leads to the development of Hope. Hope is the enduring belief that one's wishes are attainable. Failure to develop hope leads to fundamental insecurity and may compromise the ability to deal with challenges in later stages.

Stage Two – *Autonomy* versus *shame* and *doubt*. This stage occurs in the toddler and preschool years where the challenge is to balance a child's need for self-control with a parent's demand for control. Shame occurs with the loss of self-respect when the child doesn't live up to standards. The virtue of Will, the capacity to freely make choices based on realsitic expectations, is a successful outcome of this stage.

Stage Three – *Initiative* versus *guilt*. This stage occurs in the preschool years and involves the balance between taking autonomous initiative without moving outside the bounds of the parent's expectations. Successful accomplishment of this stage will result in the virtue of Purpose.

Stage Four – *Industry* versus *inferiority*. This stage occurs when children start school and must begin to achieve competencies, which, if not mastered, lead to feelings of inferiority. Thus Competence is the virtue of the fourth stage.

Stage Five – *Identity* versus *role confusion*. This stage occurs at the onset of puberty and the psychosocial changes that accompany adolescence. Identity involves a reliable, integrated sense of "who one is," based on many different roles. Role confusion leads to a failure to achieve this integration of roles. Successful resolution of this stage results in the virtue of Fidelity.

Stage Six – *Intimacy* versus *isolation*. Young adults must develop the ability to establish close committed relationships with others and cope with the fear of losing their identity and sense of self, which true intimacy requires. Love is the resulting virtue.

Stage Seven – *Generativity* versus *stagnation*. This stage, which occurs in middle adulthood, involves the successful resolution of a personally satisfying and socially meaningful life, with the stagnation that occurs when life has no purpose. If mastered, the virtue of Care results.

Stage Eight – *Ego* versus *despair*. In late adulthood, if individuals can look back on their lives with dignity and optimism, rather than despair, it will result in the virtue of Wisdom.

of each stage, conflicts from earlier stages may continue to affect later stages of development.

Stage theory ~ also known as *developmental* or *life-span theory* ~ describes and attempts to understand the predictable and behavioral changes that take place as individuals transition from one of these phases to another. Each of these stages has a particularly distinct set of definitional characteristics and challenges to be mastered before moving to another stage.

And thus, stage theory is also referred to as the *normative crisis model.* The normative crisis model assumes developmental changes occur in distinct stages, and that these stages occur over a lifetime in qualitative patterns unique one from another. The normative model further assumes that each stage is increasingly more complex while integrating to some extent or another the changes and accomplishments of earlier stages.[x]

Lifecycle Capacity Benefits

There are at least five benefits of the lifecycle approach to nonprofit capacity.

- Understanding an organization's lifecycle stage establishes a *diagnostic starting point* for capacity-building activities and helps us respond appropriately to the organization's behavior.

- A stage-based approach helps set *realistic expectations* for the "typical" behavior one might expect, on average, to find in nonprofit organizations at a specific stage.

- Knowledge of the typical characteristics of each stage helps us recognize when *behaviors are out of sync* from what might otherwise be expected at that phase of life.

- Understanding stage-based development helps *depersonalize organizational management weaknesses* and reframe current stage-related growing pains as predictable for that developmental stage.

- Finally, understanding stage-based development helps foundations, consultants and others become *more effective advocates* for the individuals or organizations they care about.

Like any analogy, the application of stage-based, lifecycle theory to nonprofits (or any organization for that matter) has its shortcomings and caveats. Before presenting the seven lifecycle stages in the next chapter, I want to acknowledge three general critiques of the lifecycle approach, which, if not understood, may lead to misapplication.

A *stage* is a developmental period when characteristic patterns of behavior are evidenced and certain capacities become established. The *stage model of development* assumes that developmental changes occur in distinct stages, and that these stages occur over a lifetime in qualitative patterns unique one from another. The normative model further assumes that each stage is increasingly more complex while integrating, to some extent or another, the changes and accomplishments of earlier stages.

- *Unlike humans, organizations do not necessarily progress through sequential stages of growth and development.* Indeed, some authors argue that lifecycle progression, rather than occurring in stages, may happen in "surges" which are neither orderly nor progressive.[xi] However, the biological or evolutionary metaphor is consistent with the all-too-frequent fact that many nonprofits, like humans, fail to mature, are forced to grow up too soon, or die a premature death.

- *Many lifecycle models do not include stages of decline or disengagement.* With notable exceptions,[xii] most economic lifecycle models, otherwise focussed on growth, seldom discuss the subjects of disengagement and decline. At any stage, organizations may intentionally disengage or unintentionally stall due to lack of desire or lack of capacity to take the next step.

- *Lifecycle models can appear deterministic rather than dynamic.* Like any diagnostic model, if you use it to judge, rather than understand, you will have missed the intent.

- *As organizations change, they frequently find themselves operating between stages.* Life "between the cracks" of one stage to another can be a very frustrating time for any organization committed to change and improvement, but still saddled with operating systems or personnel who have not yet caught up with the forward momentum. Managing and governing between the cracks is particularly difficult and can result in a two-steps forward, one-step back phenomenon. Savvy leadership keeps all eyes on progressive movement, while gradually correcting barriers to progress.

Armed then with an understanding of the roots of developmental stage theory, as well as its cautions for use, let us now introduce the seven stages of nonprofit capacity.

FOR LIFECYCLE ENTHUSIASTS ONLY

Readers with a further interest in the lifecycle approach might be interested in Larry Greiner's excellent application of lifecycle theory to organizational development. Greiner's seminal work *Evolution and Revolution as Organizations Grow* (1972, 1998)[xiii] describes five stages of evolution and revolution that, along with dimensions of age, size, and growth rate of the industry, shape an organization's development. His revolution stages are reminiscent of Erikson's normative crisis model, and indeed, Greiner uses crisis phraseology to describe the revolutionary dynamic that must be mastered.

Each of Greiner's five stages are sequential, although not automatic, and each is a result of the previous phase and a cause for the next phase. I summarize his stages here with the *Harvard Business Review*'s permission.

Phase One: *Creativity.* In the birth phase, emphasis is on creating both a product and a market. Founders are technically- or entrepreneurially-oriented and generally disdain management activities. Communication is informal and long hours of work are rewarded by modest salaries. Revolution happens when founders find themselves burdened by unwanted management responsibilities and long for the "good old days." This *crisis of leadership* is the first organizational revolution and must be resolved before moving to the next stage.

Phase Two: *Direction.* Organizations that survive the first phase now have a functional organizational structure, budgets, and accounting systems. Communication becomes more formal and impersonal and a hierarchy of titles and positions grows. All decisions rest with management, which is now somewhat more diversified. Revolution in this stage emerges from a *crisis of autonomy* when lower level employees find themselves restricted by a cumbersome and centralized hierarchy. To successfully maneuver through this stage, senior management must successfully delegate responsibility to lower level managers who otherwise will become disenchanted and leave.

Phase Three: *Delegation.* This phase is characterized by a decentralized organizational structure in which managers are given greater responsibility, profit centers and bonuses are used as motivational devices, and top management has little role in the day-to-day functioning of the organization. In the delegation phase, managers are highly motivated to operate autonomously and can become parochial in their approach, leading to the *crisis of control* in which top management seeks to regain control over the company as a whole. Companies that emphasize coordination rather than a return to centralized control will emerge to the fourth stage.

Phase Four: *Coordination.* In this phase, formalized systems are introduced to achieve greater coordination and top management leads the charge for the implementation of these systems for the company's greater good. Formal planning procedures are established, headquarters staff are hired to carry out company-wide tasks, and product groups and divisions are treated as investment centers with expectations of return on investment. All these co-ordinative efforts prove useful for achieving efficient use of company resources. Revolution occurs at this stage when systems lead to a red-tape attitude among divisional managers and staff, who increasingly resent direction from those not familiar with local conditions. If not managed, this crisis will cause serious morale problems resulting in *stagnation.*

Phase Five: *Collaboration.* Phase five's evolution is characterized by a flexible and behavioral approach to organizational management. Rather than bureaucratic red-tape, management focuses on strong interpersonal, collaborative teamwork with an emphasis on working across functions to fix problems quickly. In this phase, headquarters staff are reduced in numbers or reassigned into interdisciplinary, matrix type teams that consult with, rather than direct, field units. Greiner states that this is the phase in which many U.S. companies are currently engaged, and consequently the fifth stage revolution has yet to appear. If pressed, he suspects that the revolution will come from the psychological exhaustion that accompanies the intensity of teamwork.

3

SEVEN STAGES
OF NONPROFIT CAPACITY

People are where they are. To help them means meeting them right there ~ not where you wish they were, where they should be, nor where they tell you they are ~ but, rather, right where they are.

Gisela Konopka

Lifecycle theory assumes that organizations, like living organisms, develop through a process starting with conception and birth, and then may cycle through phases of growth, maturity, sometimes regeneration, and, eventual death. Similar to human development, some organizations die in infancy, others possess a maturity well beyond their years, while still others, despite their age, never seem to grow up.

NONPROFIT LIFECYCLES presents seven organizational stages, starting with a founding *idea,* which, in some cases converts into a *start-up* organization, or may move immediately into *terminal.* Having started, some organizations move onto the *growth stage,* while others will remain in *start-up* behaviors forever. Organizations that master the multiple challenges of the *growth stage* will eventually become *mature* organizations, although many stall in their *growth-stage* development because the challenges are greater than they have the capacity to handle.

Mature organizations need to maintain an active community connection to stay vibrant. Nonprofits that don't stay connected slip into *decline,* the stage where organizations that have rested on their laurels become status quo and out of touch. *Decliners* that catch themselves early enough may regenerate or *turn around.* Those that run out of market need, energy, or will, become *terminal.*

Figure 1: Seven Nonprofit Lifecycle Stages

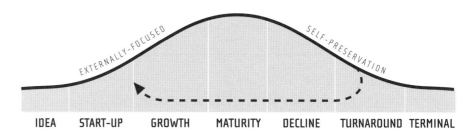

| IDEA | START-UP | GROWTH | MATURITY | DECLINE | TURNAROUND | TERMINAL |

The upside of the lifecycle curve represents the four stages where non-profits are most attuned to the community and to the needs of their constituents: *idea, start-up, growth* and *maturity*. The downside of the curve, particularly *decline* and *terminal*, reflects an inward, self-preservational focus, rather than the external orientation of the earlier stages.

Although each stage has important tasks to accomplish, *maturity* is the optimal operational stage. Until maturity is achieved, a variety of structural problems, or growing pains, will predictably distract from mission fulfillment. Growing pains are a natural part of organizational evolution, but they can frequently become stalling points and thus account for the reason that many nonprofits never reach maturity.

Once a healthy organization reaches *maturity*, the need to maintain its competitive edge and vibrancy requires continual strategic program additions and deletions. In this way, *mature* organizations oscillate between growth and *maturity* to stay vibrant.

Lifecycle Prerequisites

As you read through the stage descriptions on the following pages, keep the following things in mind:

- *There is no "exact" number of lifecycle stages.* My work with nonprofits has identified seven stages of development, but other respected authors cite four stages,[xiv] five stages,[xv] and ten stages.[xvi] The fact is there is no exact number. If after reading through this chapter you want to add or sub-divide a stage, you will get no argument from me. My intent is not to defend the number of stages, or the bell-curve depiction, but rather to persuade all nonprofits, grantmakers, researchers and management scholars that there can be no definition of nonprofit capacity without a stage-based approach.

- *The lifecycle model is diagnostic, not deterministic.* It is meant to identify an organization's capacity starting point, and by virtue of the placement, understand the dynamic stage-related challenges organizations face at that lifecycle stage.

- *The lifecycle model is not necessarily sequential nor evolutionary.* Not all organizations go through all stages, nor, if they do move from one stage to another, is the movement sequential. Many organizations move from *start-up* to *terminal.* Others, despite thirty years in business, never leave the *start-up stage.*

- *The nonprofit lifecycle model is not age or size dependent.* Rather it assumes that there are a series of predictable tasks to be accomplished at each of seven discrete stages, along with a set of stage-appropriate expectations to be fulfilled.

- *The lifecycle model is holistic.* It assumes there are multiple infrastructure requirements necessary to manage, govern, fund, and build durable systems in support of a nonprofit's programs. These infrastructural requirements, or *capacity builders,* give specific texture and form to each of the seven stages. They work together to create the multiple, complex, but predictable tasks and outcomes every nonprofit must face and master at each stage of operations.

- *It is a long way from start-up to maturity, and there are few, if any, shortcuts.* It is also an expensive road, particularly in the *growth stage* when capacity development usually begins in earnest.

- *The more advanced an organization is in its lifecycle development, the more that can be expected of it.* Thus grantmakers, board members, and even staff should be able to have higher expectations of a *mature* organization than they would of a *start-up.*

- *The lifecycle challenge is to achieve balance or complete alignment among programs, management, governance, resources, and systems at each stage.* Until balance is reached, the "stalled" capacity point will continually hold the organization back. Efforts to press on with mission or new programs will wobble, generally not because of missed market demand or opportunity, but because of structural management, governance, financial, or system weaknesses.

My intent is not to defend the number of stages, or the bell-curve depiction, but rather to persuade all nonprofits, grantmakers, researchers and management scholars that there can be no definition of nonprofit capacity without a stage-based approach.

Nonprofit Lifecycle Stages at a Glance

Stage #1: Idea
The stage in which there is no formal organization, only an idea and a personal mandate to fill a societal, programmatic or cultural gap in the community.

Stage #2: Start-Up
The beginning stage of organizational operations in which unbridled mission, energy, and passion reign supreme, but, generally, without corresponding governance, management, resources, or systems.

Stage #3: Growth
The stage in which nonprofit mission and programs have taken hold in the marketplace, but where service demand exceeds current structural and resource capabilities.

Stage #4: Maturity
The stage of operation in which the organization is well-established, operating smoothly, and has a community reputation for providing consistently relevant and high quality services.

Stage #5: Decline
The stage in which the organization's services are no longer relevant to the marketplace, self-indulgent, status-quo decisions are made, and declining program census creates insufficient operating income to cover expenses.

Stage #6: Turnaround
The stage at which an organization, having faced a critical juncture due to lost market share and revenues, takes decisive action to reverse prior actions in a self-aware, determined manner.

Stage #7: Terminal
The stage when an organization has neither the will, purpose nor energy to continue to exist.

THE SEVEN STAGES OF NONPROFIT CAPACITY

The Idea Stage: The Magnificent Obsession

The stage in which there is no formal organization, only an idea and a personal mandate to fill a societal, programmatic, or cultural gap in the community.

The lifecycle model assumes that all organizations begin with an idea, and in nonprofit organizations, this idea is someone's vision of what could or should be, if only the right circumstances prevailed. Most nonprofit ideas reflect a founding perception of a societal or cultural vacuum and a personal mandate to do something about it.

Founding ideas may incubate for years before becoming fledgling organizations, or they may be launched into reality in a relatively compressed timeframe, if timing is right, and the demand compelling.

In many ways the *idea stage* is like an all-consuming hobby. It occupies a lot of time and requires substantial commitment on the part of its originators without corresponding financial or material reward. It is only when the idea is shared with others that outside possibilities and expectations begin to surface, and the *idea stage* formally begins.

Ideas do not happen without people, and in that way they are completely dependent on the energy and enthusiasm of their creators. The *idea stage*, although the most infectious, is also the most fragile. If the originator loses enthusiasm or fails to mobilize others, the idea will not be convertible. Although the vision, hopes, and dreams of the conceptualizer are essential, founders at this stage of development neither understand what they are doing nor how they will handle future hurdles. However, they are very clear, and often messianic, about the *why* of their venture.

Founding ideas are generally brought to life with little or no money. Unless the originators themselves have deep pockets, or are able to enlist the support of an outside "angel," the founding idea is usually conceived with nothing more than the sweat equity of the founder and a band of eager supporters.

CHALLENGES OF THE IDEA STAGE

- Identifying an unmet need

- Developing mission and vision

- Mobilizing the support of others

- Converting the idea into action

In many ways the *idea stage* is like an all-consuming hobby. It occupies a lot of time and requires substantial commitment on the part of its originators without corresponding financial or material reward. It is only when the idea is shared with others that outside possibilities and expectations begin to surface, and the *idea stage* formally begins.

27

The Start-up Stage: The Labor of Love

The beginning stage of organizational operations in which unbridled mission, energy, and passion reign supreme, but generally without corresponding governance, management, resources or systems.

At the point when a nonprofit idea becomes incorporated as an organization, the *idea stage* ends and *start-up* begins.

The *start-up* stage is characterized by high energy, and strong dependence on the vision of the founder(s). Unless otherwise seeded by a large, progenitive grant, the *start-up stage* is almost always characterized by the proverbial "shoestring budget."

Start-ups run on unbridled passion, and a do-or-die commitment to get their services to the marketplace. They are always open to opportunity and to yet another chance to tell people about their passionate commitment to their cause.

In the early years, *start-ups* generally have a strong ideology from which they create programs and services. Disillusionment can set in, though, when strong beliefs meet the realities of outside constituents and funders. Nonetheless, *start-up* founders know how to create a spirit of excitement in their staff, board members, clients, and community, developing them into loyal constituents, capable of sharing the founding dream and the work it will take to accomplish it.

Although the fledgling organization may be dependent on originators for its continued care and feeding, once a nonprofit is formed, the founder legally becomes just one of several interested parties. This is one of the crucial differences between nonprofit corporations and small businesses that, similarly, begin with a founding idea. In a small business, especially those incorporated as sole-proprietorships, the founder owns the business. Nonprofit founders, at least in concept, relinquish organizational ownership the day tax-exempt status is attained.

When an organization is incorporated as tax-exempt, *the nonprofit belongs to the community,* represented by a board of directors. Due diligence responsibilities require nonprofit board members to govern, monitor, and safeguard the organization as if it were their own, thus relieving the founder in another way from sole responsibility or "ownership" of the nonprofit entity.

The nonprofit founder is generally a personable, charismatic, and inspirational leader, but just as often, may not be a good manager. This is easily forgiven in the *start-up stage,* when energy and commitment take precedence to management and operations.

The board of directors of a *start-up* nonprofit often functions more like a loose-knit band of supporters and advisors than in a textbook governance role. They probably also serve as unpaid staff or program volunteers. Although legally responsible for the success or failure of the organization, they are often the last to know it.

Frequently *start-up* boards are comprised of constituents, personal friends, or supporters of the founder, who themselves, have some personal connection to the mission.

The role of a nonprofit board at any lifecycle stage is to set direction and to govern. But in the *start-up* stage, especially in circumstances where board members have been recruited by the founder, a board member often has difficulty assuming the rightful governance role. Board members get confused about to whom the organization "belongs" and may think of it as a sole-proprietorship, belonging to the founder, rather than a nonprofit corporation meant for the betterment of the community.

The ideal *start-up* board is comprised of multi-talented individuals who are both committed to the mission and willing to roll up their shirtsleeves to tackle what needs to be done. Sometimes this means serving as the bookkeeper for the fledgling nonprofit. Other times board members fill in as fundraisers, mail stuffers, or marketing people ~ all perfectly appropriate roles in the *start-up* stage where money and staff are in short supply. It is only as the nonprofit moves into later stages where this type of hands-on involvement becomes inappropriate, and indeed troublesome, if the board member can't let go of tasks and move onto governance.

Start-up founders and board members are aided by *first-staff* who, similar to the founder and original board, usually have a personal link to the organization's social cause or artistic endeavor.

First staff need to be flexible, "can-do" individuals, since they will surely wear many hats and play multiple organizational roles during the development stage. For that reason, it is often wiser in the *start-up* stage to hire versatile generalists rather than more narrowly-skilled technicians.

First staff are a treasure and should be chosen wisely since, along with the founder, they will play a big role in shaping the nonprofit's future. First staff are generally as loyal and willing to support the mission of the founder as they are to roll with the inevitable punches which go with the beginning phase of operations. They must thrive on chaos and enjoy the thrill of never knowing what tomorrow will bring. And since there is an inverse relationship between work and money at this stage, they also must be willing to work long hours with low pay.

Start-ups have a do-or-die commitment to getting their service to the

In the early years, *start-ups* generally have a strong ideology from which they create programs and services. *Start-up* founders know how to create a spirit of excitement in their staff, board members, clients, and community, developing them into loyal constituents, capable of sharing the founding dream and the work it will take to accomplish it.

marketplace. They're always open to opportunity and consequently may not know when to say "no." One could argue *start-ups* don't dare say "no," since, in this phase, you never know when another opportunity will come around the corner. The programs and services of *start-ups* tend to be simple and experimental, and, at least in the beginning, with less depth than breadth as they test what works and what doesn't.

Financially, the *start-up* organization is usually a low-budget, bootstrap operation whose main financial challenge is to live within its means, whether cash or in-kind. This usually means operating on a cash budget and learning to master the timing of cash flow payouts with expected receipts. Audits and full monthly financial statements, although fundamental tools for later stages of development, are often premature to any *start-up* whose only asset is cash.

But not all *start-ups* begin life without cash. Some nonprofits are the product of a foundation initiative or collaborative in which mega-dollars are committed at the outset to solve a local or national problem. In the earlier edition of this book I referred to this as "progenitive funding" but, thanks to Katharine Peck, a foundation colleague in Denver, I now have a new name for this type of *start-up*, "start-ups on steroids."

Nonprofits that begin life with a significant cash investment are generally able to pull their capacity pieces together much quicker than start-ups without cash because, along with the cash, they can generally recruit more experienced community board members and pay for senior level, experienced staff. In other words, they can pay for capacity earlier in the game than most other nonprofits. The critical time-period comes when the first traunch of funds sunsets and the organization must now seek a second set of funders, frequently different from the progenitors. At this point, even *start-ups on steroids* need to become entrepreneurial and start selling their mission just like those nonprofits that start without cash. Two things make this task even harder: when the program is so closely tied to the original funder(s) that others can't see themselves picking up the mantle; or, when the original executive is a content expert rather than a fund-raiser or entrepreneurial type.

In any case, starting on steroids, although arguably easier than starting without progenitive funding, will generally buy the organization about 5-7 years before they will face many of the same lifecycle challenges experienced by other *start-ups*.

By nature of the stage, *start-ups*, whether started from scratch or on steroids, are always doing things for the first time, and generally have neither the time nor the inclination to systematize activities, since all their energy goes to getting their services into the community. The old adage about "operating out of a shoe box" is truer than most *start-ups* would like to admit, at least in the beginning.

The very nature of their activities keep *start-ups* in continual motion, frequent chaos and sometimes crisis ~ yet energy and dedication push them on toward their goals. One nonprofit executive described this period in his organization's history as the "insane adventure."

Sad, but true, many nonprofits never leave the *start-up* stage. For some it is an ideological issue: they believe that nonprofit organizations are meant to be high energy, low budget operations. But for others, failure to progress beyond *start-up* is a result of not mastering the predictable growing pains attendant to the *start-up* stage.

CHALLENGES OF THE START-UP STAGE

- Sharing vision and organizational responsibility with staff, board and constituencies

- Knowing when to say "no"

- Hiring versatile staff

- Leveraging sweat equity into outside support

- Living within financial means

> In the *growth stage*, nonprofits develop distinctive competence, the factor that distinguishes them from others and provides a basis for internal pride and external support. Later, if successful at positioning this competence in the marketplace, distinctive competence becomes the reputation that thrusts the nonprofit into *maturity*.

The Growth Stage: Becoming Who You Are
The stage in which nonprofit mission and programs have taken hold in the marketplace, but where service demand exceeds current structural and resource capabilities.

Nonprofits enter the *growth stage* when their services have been embraced by the community and, to keep up with demand, their only choice is to expand. In some cases, expanding is a planned activity accomplished through adherence to a business plan, but as frequent as not, growth just "happens." There is nothing strategic about it.

In many ways, the *growth stage* is a transitional period between the stages of *start-up* and *maturity*. Although much has been written about the difficulties that accompany managing a *start-up*, it is really the *growth stage* that is the more complex management challenge. The *growth stage* is the nonprofit's adolescence, lifecycle theory's acknowledgement that, to successfully mature, organizations, too, need time to test their wings as they become who they are.

A nonprofit's *growth stage*, although a period of perpetual motion, is really a means to an end. It is the stage in which, by definition, demand for service exceeds the organization's management, board, resource and/or systems capabilities. In the lifecycle model, "growth" forces nonprofits to deal effectively (through continued adherence to mission) and efficiently (through development of internal systems) with the wider array of services they, by now, have undertaken.

In the *growth stage*, organizations begin to define their mission and service niche more carefully. A *start-up* nonprofit is willing to do almost anything to prove that its services can and should exist. But "proving it" is the *start-up's* challenge while "focusing" becomes the operative challenge for *growth-stagers*. With focusing comes increased attention to the values, service, and delivery mechanisms that set this nonprofit apart from its peers.

Growth-stagers spend a considerable amount of energy creating and refining a style that distinguishes their service from that of others, and through this refinement they discover their "distinctive competence." Distinctive competence assumes the nonprofit is good at something that the community wants or needs, and that part of what makes them good is the *style* in which they perform the service. Erik Erikson refers to an analogous process in personal development as a period of "separateness transcended" or "distinctiveness confirmed."

In the *growth stage*, as nonprofits become more deeply aware of what makes them who they are, they begin to further refine service in such a way that, organizationally, they become less dependent on individuals and more method-oriented. Thus a distinctive style which might have been developed by or associated with an individual staff person gives way to an "approach" or a "methodology" that is now transformed into an organizational hallmark, or "brand."

Clients coming for service or programs know what services they can expect and the style and approach in which the service will be delivered. Without distinctive competence, a nonprofit has no means to distinguish itself from its peers. Thus, distinctive competence becomes a nonprofit's "edge" and provides a distinguishing factor for internal pride and external support. Later, if successful at positioning this competence in the marketplace, distinctive competence becomes the reputation that brands the nonprofit and thrusts it into maturity.

As the quest for competence occurs, *growth-stage* managers find themselves increasingly frustrated by their heretofore "Jack or Jill of all trades" management style. So they begin to experiment with structural models that bring a new set of specialized skills to the organization and often become the nonprofit's first introduction to strategic divisions of labor. In my experience, this attempt to formalize job positions and responsibilities is perhaps the biggest human relations challenge a nonprofit will ever face. (See Chapter 8 for a case example of this critical juncture) In the transition from *start-up* to *growth* a peculiar phenomenon occurs: staff who have worked so hard to build something together now realize they have something to lose. This realization brings about many behavioral changes as first staff, too, learn to evolve with the organization.

Original staff members frequently dislike the organization as it begins to formalize. A group that once operated as a small, relaxed family is now beset with personnel policies, filing systems, accountabilities, and monthly staff meetings. Staff in this stage become less forgiving of the founder or organizational leader, and begin to question "why," often for the first time. They get weary of the long hours yet don't want to relinquish cherished duties ~ they "used to like working here" but "now it has started to feel like just a job."

The addition of new staff also creates havoc with the nonprofit's once informal, familiar communication style. In the *start-up* stage, there were few if any information boundaries. But as new staff are added, roles become clearer and more distinct. Likewise, skill requirements become better defined and the chain of communication moves toward a "need to know" basis. This can be a very disconcerting time for staff and the nonprofit as a whole.

Early employees who were loyal, energetic partners now feel displaced by "professional" staff who don't know the program as well as they do, nor all it took to get there. In short, in the *growth stage*, skill and specialization supplant organizational virtues of loyalty and willingness that served the nonprofit so well in *start-up*. This can bring tremendous grief to both the manager who realizes that a long-term employee's skills no longer match what's needed at this stage of development and to the employee who is on the receiving end of this news.

Usually no one is more ambivalent about the changes necessitated by the *growth stage* than the founder. Founders, or any *growth-stage* manager for that matter, although understanding the need for structure and desperately wanting to see their ideas reach *maturity*, are often caught in the trap of getting energized through crisis management. They may not be able to bring themselves to replace under-skilled but loyal staff with more competence. This is a very critical turning point in a nonprofit's development. If not handled correctly, it could mean a major stalling point for the organization, a stall from which many nonprofits never recover.

Staff burnout is another predictable by-product of the *growth-stage*. Founders and other staff get tired of fighting the same battles, yet they are bored with the prospect of routine. As systems get organized, some founders decide they liked it better when things were not so routinized.

Growth-stage boards of directors are not immune to the changes occurring in the organization either. Things happen so fast in this stage that members, who in *start-up* could miss several meetings, now find themselves out of the loop if they don't attend on a regular basis.

In the *growth stage*, boards of directors begin to transition from being a support group for the founder to accepting responsibility for the organization. This often means recruiting additional professional expertise to the board to augment the expertise and personal affiliations of many *start-up* board members.

New board members, like new staff, will have increased expectations of how the board should function. The *growth stage* is the period when boards begin to establish terms of office, formalize meeting times and correspondence, and institute committee structures. It is the stage when the board too becomes more professional. But increased professionalism should not in any way diminish commitment to mission. Executive directors or nominating committees recruiting new members to a *growth-stage* nonprofit must remember to orient and acquaint new officers with the organization's mission so that later financial, legal, personnel, or other decisions can be made in the context of organizational purpose rather than just operational expediency.

The opportunities and challenges of the *growth-stage* requires board members who are not only committed experts, but also people with the capacity to make informed decisions in an expeditious fashion. Opportunity knocks incessantly on the door of the *growth-stage* nonprofit. Board members must be prepared to deal with opportunities as they come. Too much tabling and studying sends opportunity packing. *Growth stage* board members are expert enough to understand market conditions and quick enough on the draw to decide if, when, and how an opportunity fits within the future of their organization.

Ultimately, the true test of the board of a growing nonprofit is its willingness to understand its governance role. The board's own *growth-stage* challenge is to transition itself from a group of individuals formed to support the executive director to a governing body who realizes that, by law, they are charged with monitoring the ultimate success or failure of the organization.

For this reason, the most important ally an executive director can have in the *growth stage* is a board chair who understands the organization's mission as well as its developing structural challenges. A board chair who can oversee the work of the board and support the executive's efforts at building institutional capacity frees the executive to focus on programmatic and operational work. Achieving a true partnership between the board chair and the executive director is an important milestone of the *growth stage*, and often an important first step in fostering board ownership without which the board will never achieve maturity. (See *Chapter 7: Developing Board Ownership*.)

As if the human dynamics of the *growth stage* weren't enough, nonprofits in the *growth stage* are generally chronically undercapitalized. They are always playing catch up, and though their product or service is in demand, *growth-stage*rs continually struggle to find the right product mix to serve their artistic or service destiny.

Financially, *growth* is the stage when management and boards begin to see the necessity for monthly statements that track financial performance. No longer does the budget suffice as the sole-source financial document. Financial statements ~ audits, balance sheets, and income statements ~ provide the current status of the nonprofit's assets, liabilities, and net assets (fund balances) as well as an actual recap of monthly income and expense. Cash flow projections, particularly for revenue-based operations, are also a critical financial management tool. The more strapped a nonprofit is for cash, the more helpful cash flow projections will be.

The *growth stage* is proportionally the most expensive stage in any nonprofit's development. It is the phase when staff salaries begin to be upgraded; previously donated space now requires payment; bookkeepers or accountants are hired; computers, copy machines and phone systems are purchased; and audits are done for the first time. Consequently, it is not uncommon for the administrative expense category to take a disproportionate bite out of the *growth-stage* nonprofit's budget. Although nobody relishes allocating hard-earned dollars to administrative items, if these needs are not attended to, they will retard the organization's future abilities to mature. Far too many important nonprofits are stalled in the *growth stage* because of inadequate systems or untrained administrative staff, which end up costing the organization more than it saves by failing to upgrade appropriately.

Time, above all else, is the *growth-stage* organization's biggest enemy. Effective growth managers are good time managers and they encourage efficient use of time in their staff and board members too. When delegating a job, they place deadlines or check-in points on the project, or they say "this project is only worth two hours" so that staff get a sense of the project's priority.

Although all stages have their challenges, it is the *growth stage*, with its complexity of services, but lack of structure, that leads management and board members to the feeling that they are burning the candle at both ends.

CHALLENGES OF THE GROWTH STAGE

• Too much to do, too little time

• Developing board ownership

• Creating a program and strategic focus that does not trap creativity and vision

• Identifying distinctive competence

• Beginning to formalize organizational structure

• Becoming comfortable with change

• Diversifying revenues and managing cash flow

The Maturity Stage: Maintaining Your Edge

The stage of operation in which the organization is well-established, operating smoothly, and has a community reputation for providing consistently relevant and high quality services.

The move from the *growth stage* to *maturity* occurs when five conditions have been met:

• Services are firmly recognized and identified in the marketplace

• There is a mutual sense of organizational ownership between the executive and the board

• A financial backbone of support and revenue has been achieved

• Administrative systems are at or near the level of sophistication required for competent program delivery, management, and decision-making, and

• If the founder is still in place, he or she has effectively separated his/her own personal identity from that of the organization. (See Chapter 6 for case illustration)

Mature nonprofits have built their brand and community reputation around excellent, dependable services that are multi-dimensional and more comprehensive than at former stages. Nobody questions whether the *mature* nonprofit will be around tomorrow. Neither is there hesitancy about competence. When the nonprofit's name is mentioned, there is immediate name recognition and a sense of what the organization does.

The *mature* organization knows its clients and its clients know them. *Mature* nonprofits have built their brand and community reputation around excellent excellent, reliable services that are usually multi-dimensional and more comprehensive than at earlier stages.

The *mature* nonprofit is viewed as a leader among its peers. Management and staff time is set aside for industry-related service. Key staff serve on the boards of directors of industry-related membership groups or task forces. In this way, the *mature*, established organization participates in the development of its field.

Mature nonprofits also engage in public policy and education on topics related to their mission. Unlike the earlier stages when time is a premium, the established organization keeps abreast and seeks to influence public policy based on its own wealth of experience.

Mature organizations have well-functioning boards of directors that are policy driven and understand their legal and fiduciary responsibilities. Board meetings are well-orchestrated, agendas come out ahead of time and clearly state the business to be discussed and the decisions to be made.

The *mature* board of directors has a stable membership with rotating terms of office. Its composition may reflect a diversity of competence, gender, culture, position, and age. The board plays a leadership role, has the competence to understand the pressing issues facing the organization, and advises the executive director accordingly.

Mature boards of directors govern. They don't expect to roll up their shirt sleeves and engage in operational tasks. Although not as familiar with the day-to-day operations as they used to be, they understand it is no failure on their part that they no longer know the names or circumstances of all staff. They set or approve overall organizational direction and leave the management to the executive director.

By now, the *mature* organization has evened-out its management and staffing issues. There is executive leadership who often is second or third generation from the founder. Executive directors of *mature* nonprofits understand and enjoy managing. They know that their role is to provide stable, predictable services in keeping with community needs and resources. Consequently, *mature* executives need to anticipate and thwart internal and external crises. They must be excellent motivators. Above all, they need to inspire and maintain the community's confidence.

Conventional wisdom and the popular press suggest that the original founder, usually a hard-driving visionary, may not be well-suited to the even-keeled management requirements of the *mature* nonprofit corporation, and in many individual cases this is certainly true. But probing the literature further supports my consulting experience that the key to whether or not a founder will be able to grow to *maturity* with the nonprofit lies in the founder's understanding and willingness to master the skills required to manage a *mature* organization. For most founders, this means unlearning years of habits that made them successful in the earlier stages. It also means separating their own needs for personal stimulation from the organization's needs, and this may prove a bitter pill to swallow for someone who for years has relied on the organization for personal satisfaction and stimulation.[xvii]

Whether founder or not, by *maturity*, the executive director now has a more seasoned staff, people to whom most program, financial and administrative functions can be delegated. This staff is by now a mix of old and new, many of whom are professionals with reputations of their own. They are usually credentialed and, if not well-compensated, at least paid better than they were in the earlier lifecycle stages.

Staff in the *mature stage* expect things to run smoothly. They become reliant on routine schedules. They often have their own private offices and now communicate by memo, e-mail, and conferences, rather than the informal spur of the moment updates used in earlier stages.

In this stage, management begins to think about enhancing benefit packages for employees. Attention is paid to enrichment opportunities that would have been out of the question in the cash-poor days of *start-up* or *growth*. It is not uncommon for *mature* organizations to have retirement plans, paid sick leave, employer paid medical benefits, life insurance, and even severance packages. And this is possible because, by now, *mature* organizations have an ongoing source of funding that can be counted on for the majority of income requirements. Government contracts, reliable sales, the United Way, a membership base, or a pool of established donors may provide this financial backbone depending on the nonprofit's field of service.

Mature organizations are able to weather the ebbs and flows that accompany the fund-raising process. Since their budgets are larger than at earlier periods, they can often make adjustments to expense projections when anticipated income doesn't materialize. While financially healthy

Mature nonprofits know who they are and have successfully positioned themselves in the community. They know how to maintain their distinctive competence, the "edge," that made them successful in the first place. Even though they have abandoned the entrepreneurial management styles that were appropriate to earlier stages of development, they have not lost touch with the needs of the community or the willingness to take advantage of market opportunities. In fact, they keep an ever-watchful eye out for changing community trends and needs.

nonprofits have learned not to run a deficit, if an occasional operating shortfall does occur, there are quite often surpluses gained from prior periods which can cover shortfalls.

Mature organizations have adequate financial tracking and control systems that inform management and boards on where they stand financially and what course corrections may be indicated. Financially healthy organizations equate deficits with poor management practice, knowing that, by running a deficit, the organization precludes itself from starting new programs or staying in control of its own destiny.

In the *mature stage*, management and boards begin to develop the organization's fund balances. Up until now, most energy has been focused on developing sufficient income to meet growing operating needs. *Mature* nonprofits understand the wisdom of building internal financial capacity into its annual budget to ensure programmatic and organizational vitality.

Thus *mature* organizations begin to build operating reserve funds through the accumulation of prior period surpluses or through designated foundation gifts. Some establish endowments during this period. Either way, the prudent board of directors will require that these reserve or endowment funds be segregated from the corporation's operating assets so that they not be eroded in day-to-day activities.

In the *mature stage*, nonprofits become more policy-oriented. Personnel policies are developed or refined, and board manuals and employee handbooks are created. Client-focused policies are developed that outline grievance procedures, conflict resolution actions, and the like. This is also the stage when a nonprofit begins to produce annual reports and brochures more reflective of program quality than the lower budget reports that may have been produced in earlier years.

Mature organizations have already experienced the trials and errors of developing efficient systems, and for the most part, they have a good handle on the variety of techniques that make for smooth operations. To be sure, few organizations can ever boast systems totally consistent with what they would like. This is especially true for *mature* but vibrant nonprofits, whose administrative practices will change based on the dynamic nature of programming.

Clearly *maturity* is the pinnacle to which all nonprofits should aspire since *mature* organizations, by definition, accomplish their missions without the distractions and growing pains of the earlier stages ~ too little time, continual cash flow problems, not enough staff, or an unreliable board, to name a few.

But *maturity* too, has its challenges, the biggest of which is to maintain its vitality so that it doesn't slip into *decline*.

Mature nonprofits know who they are and have successfully positioned themselves in the community. They know how to maintain their distinctive competence, the "edge," that made them successful in the first place. Even though they have abandoned the entrepreneurial management styles that were appropriate to earlier stages of development, they have not lost touch with the needs of the community or the willingness to take advantage of market opportunities. In fact, they keep an ever-watchful eye out for changing community trends and needs.

Above all, *mature* organizations don't take their positions for granted. They continue to look for new opportunities that enhance their existing services and fill market voids. It is common for *mature* nonprofits to have new programs running side by side with more established activities. In this way, *vibrantly mature* organizations are always oscillating between *growth* and *maturity*, thus keeping their "edge." Maintaining a sense of vibrancy results from functioning simultaneously at peak program and organizational performance as well as peak community connection and perception. Vitality, the cycling back and forth between *growth stage* and *maturity*, is the organizational "sweet spot" that many organizations enjoy and others hope to attain. (See Figure 4 on page 41)

Mature, vibrant nonprofits know who they are and have successfully positioned themselves in the community. They have reached a peak in their maturation process that they do not take for granted, for to do so will generally result in *decline*.

CHALLENGES OF THE MATURE STAGE

- Remaining client centered rather than policy bound

- Keeping staff motivated around the mission

- Building financial footings of endowment or reserves

- Maintaining their programmatic "edge," cycling programs in and out based on continued relevancy

- Becoming "position" rather than "person" dependent

The Decline Stage: Someone That You Used to Be
The stage in which an organization's services are no longer relevant to the marketplace, self-indulgent, status-quo decisions are made, and declining program census creates insufficient operating income to cover expenses.

Many nonprofits experience occasional setbacks and stress points that may feel like the beginning of "decline." Indeed, no dynamic organization, non-profit or otherwise, can escape the frequent frustrations and sometime failures that predictably occur in all of the lifecycle stages. Yet, if identified and understood, these critical moments can become healthy turning points in a nonprofit's development. Jungian psychologist Murray Stein uses the term "liminality" to describe a period of human development when identity falls apart only to reconfigure at a more complex, mature level of functioning. Although his reference is to individuals in their mid-30s and 40s, the concept is useful for nonprofits too, especially those once mature and venerable organizations who, because of changes in the marketplace, now face the need for regeneration.

Regeneration is that flash-point between *maturity* and *decline* when nonprofits, having reached *maturity* but failed to maintain their vibrancy, have a flash of insight that leads to a deeper sense of identity and re-connection to community. And there, in the willingness to face itself head-on and make necessary adaptations, lies the difference between a nonprofit in a liminal process of regeneration and one moving into *decline.*

Figure 4: Nonprofit Lifecycle Stages with *Vitality* and *Regeneration*

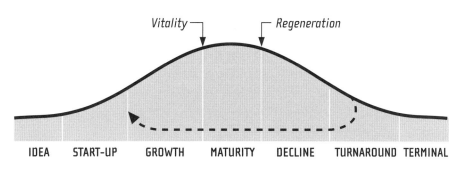

Nonprofits can enter the *decline stage* from almost any lifecycle stage, but generally the progression goes from *maturity* to *decline*, or from *start-up* to *decline.* When *start-ups* decline it is almost always because of capacity issues, frequently related to management (sometimes a founder) who is not willing to let the organization mature beyond their own personal inclinations. Thus an almost crippling paralysis ensues in which nothing changes nor can anything progress. Thus, sadly, we see organizations become "prematurely gray," never moving beyond their *start-up* capacities, instead, "tunneling" directly into *decline.*

Declining organizations are often the slowest to recognize their lifecycle stage. Whereas *start-up, growth* and *turnaround* are clearly recognizable stages, those in *decline* are easily lulled into thinking that yesterday's reality is still applicable today. For that reason, nonprofits in *decline* solve today's problems with yesterday's solutions, often focusing on the activity rather than the result.

But for nonprofits that enter *decline* having once been *mature,* the situation is different. The *decline stage* occurs when nonprofits forget the tenuous balance between mission and market. Rather than keeping an eye peeled for market needs and demands, the declining organization focuses instead on continuing its own programs and interests, usually at all costs. As the world turns around them, *decline-stage* groups, comfortable with the way things are (or were), continue to conduct business in the usual manner, oblivious to what's happening in their field or marketplace. (See Chapter 9 for a case illustration.)

Decline-stage nonprofits have an inward focus that is concerned more with staff and management needs than clients. Rigidity has set in, as the emphasis becomes "what we do and how we do it" rather than who needs it and why it's needed.

In *decline*, staff and management become locked into their own tried and true methods and seldom seek evaluative client feedback. This can result in a form of self-indulgence, that later, as the stage progresses, deteriorates into an organizational paralysis having gone so long without self-renewing activities.

Sometimes, *decline* occurs when long-term executives, by now in their fifties or sixties and mindful of impending retirement, let their organizations "coast" rather than start new initiatives in their own waning years. Although coasting into retirement might be understandable on an individual level, it is never good for an organization. Coasting leads to stagnation, and stagnation is the first step toward *decline*. So, as in all the other lifecycle stages, executives need to separate their own personal needs from the lifecycle requirements of their organizations. This is an especially timely reminder for baby-boomer executives as we begin to take leave from the nonprofit workforce.

Organizations in *decline* don't like to change. They generally have well-established programs which have taken on lives of their own, and an acquired "sacred" status, that is not easily adaptable when community or market needs begin to change. Interestingly enough, organizations in *decline* often don't have money problems, at least in the beginning. In fact, especially when organizations move into *decline* from the *mature stage,* they often do so with abundant cash reserves that soon erode as they are drawn down to cover annual operating losses.

Denial and blame usually accompany decline. Denial takes many forms, from making excuses for losing program contracts or clients, to blaming decreased funding or revenues on an outside phenomenon. Either way, rather than acknowledge and adapt to the circumstance, the organization ignores or makes excuses for it.

Declining organizations are often the slowest to recognize their lifecycle stage. Whereas *start-up*, *growth* and *turnaround* are clearly recognizable stages, those in *decline* are easily lulled into thinking that yesterday's reality is still applicable today. For that reason, nonprofits in *decline* solve today's problems with yesterday's solutions, often focusing on the activity rather than the result.

The board of directors may frequently be the last to know their nonprofit is in *decline*. From the board's perspective, things are running smoothly. They're getting their reports on time; meetings run smoothly; and the continual cash flow crises of the earlier years have now been resolved.

But when a nonprofit fails to elicit more than just governance from its board, even the most faithful board members may begin to lose interest. So board members in the *decline stage* often fail to come to meetings since they don't feel needed. In a sense the board reflects the organizational *ennui* that permeates the organization. They've lost their enthusiasm and have little to spark their continued commitment.

Still, it is generally a board member, through attention to both explicit and subtle warning signs, who ends up "blowing the whistle" on the *declining* nonprofit. And since there is generally no joy in being the bearer of bad news, whistle-blowing board members often experience more than a few moments of self-doubt, asking themselves more than once, *Am I seeing this correctly? Am I the only one who thinks something is wrong?*

It is at this stage that many boards hire an outside consultant to take stock of the situation. A savvy nonprofit consultant will quickly ascertain whether the organization is in *decline* and point it out. But with or without outside counsel, it is still the board who will need to take the steps necessary to renew itself and regain client focus. Generally the same executive director who downshifts a nonprofit into *decline* will be incapable of turning the organization back around.

There are only two ways out of the *decline stage*. If nothing changes, declining organizations will erode further into the *terminal stage*, or, through some intervention, generally from a new board member, a funder, or occasionally a staff person, it will face up to its *decline* and set the *turnaround* wheels in motion.

CHALLENGES OF THE DECLINE STAGE

- Reconnecting with community need, discarding programs that duplicate or don't add value

- Remembering that policies and procedures, systems and structure, are no substitute for creativity and risk-taking

- Keeping board members engaged

- Raising enough operating income so reserves are not drawn down for everyday use

- Examining the budget for top-heavy administrative expenses

The Turnaround Stage: Where the Rubber Meets the Road

The stage at which an organization, having faced a critical juncture due to lost market share and revenues, takes decisive action to reverse prior actions in a self-aware, determined manner.

The sixth lifecycle stage is the *turnaround stage*, probably the most exhilarating, but at the same time exhausting, of any of the lifecycle stages.

Most *turnarounds* occur when nonprofits are faced with a crisis from which they cannot escape, a crisis so big that the denial methods used in the past will no longer support the survival-threatening circumstances which now enshroud the agency.

Typically the decision to "turn around" happens at or near the crisis point ~ creditors are demanding money; venders are requiring cash on delivery; staff are mutinying. However, in the best of circumstances, the turnaround decision may occur earlier when some financial or programmatic forecast predicts that, without change, such a crisis is likely to result.

Although the *turnaround stage* ultimately involves a major restructuring of management, finances, operations and marketing strategies, to be successful, it must quickly and effectively address client and marketplace needs and relevance. This means a fundamental refocusing on both mission and market.

There are several preceding conditions symptomatic of the need for a turnaround. None of these conditions ensures that *turnaround* will occur, but they signal early warning signs of trouble.

- *Dwindling market position.* Nonprofits, like any company, lose their community position for a variety of reasons including the entrance of new competition, deterioration in service quality, or changing community demands. The first step in a successful *turnaround* is strategic restructuring ~ the process of assessing the long- and short-term needs of the community and adapting services to fit accordingly.

---

*Most *turnarounds* occur when nonprofits are faced with a crisis from which they cannot escape, a crisis so big that the denial methods used in the past will no longer support the survival-threatening circumstances which now enshroud the agency. Although the *turnaround-stage* ultimately involves a major restructuring of management, finances, operations and marketing strategies, to be successful, it must quickly and effectively address client and marketplace needs and relevance. This means a fundamental refocusing on both mission and market.*

- *Lack of financial control.* Losing control of an organization's finances, pursuing projects without sufficient revenue sources, spending according to budget without regard to income, and not paying payroll taxes all point to a lack of financial control.

- *Deterioration of physical space.* In many cases, deterioration of physical space can be symptomatic of an organization in trouble, especially if the space was once maintained with higher standards.

- *Flagging morale.* Organizational depression, paralysis, and continual crisis can result in dispirited employees who, now that the pride is gone, feel "without options" and thus have trouble generating enthusiasm for the mission and programs.

The person best suited to lead the *turnaround* is generally not the same executive manager at the helm during the *decline stage*. *Turnaround* managers are fearless, take-charge types, utterly confident of their abilities and not out to win popularity contests. They are able to quickly size up the situation, mobilize resources, and restore the confidence of the community in the mission and operations of the program. They take personal responsibility for the successful repositioning of the organization and, though reliant on facts, trust their instincts about what's needed for success.

The *turnaround* manager is a "spark-plug" who possesses absolute faith in his or her own abilities to bring the organization back into vitality. The *turnaround* manager's spark is contagious and encourages staff, constituents, venders, and funders to jump on board and do their part for the nonprofit's revitalization.

One of the toughest challenges faced by the *turnaround* manager is the revitalization of staff. Staff who have been with the nonprofit through its *decline stage* usually enter *turnaround* defeated, enmeshed, or barely "hanging-on," making restoring focus and spirit one of the first challenges. And it's an important ingredient in the successful turnaround, since *turnaround* staff, just like their manager, must be "can-do" people willing to accept the fact that things are about to be different and throw in their lot with the *turnaround* manager.

Early on, the *turnaround* manager needs to declare to all parties that the organization is in fact in a renewal period, which means a new set of expectations and behaviors on the part of all. Staff who feel out of sync with these new requirements will generally move on.

Turnaround managers take personal responsibility for the successful repositioning of the organization. Although reliant on facts, *turnaround* managers trust their instincts as to what will and won't work for the future. The turnaround manager is a risk-taker, capable of accurately seeing a problem, diagnosing its cause and then taking decisive actions resulting in effective solutions.

Sometimes this means elimination of programs or leads to replacement of tenured staff or board members. One thing is sure ~ these decisions and their impending solutions are never the easy way out.

In the *turnaround stage* the board becomes almost like a *start-up* board. Although clearly responsible for setting the repositioning goals and priorities, the actual *turnaround* is generally accomplished by the manager, in combination with a smaller number of board members, who, for a period of time, roll up their shirtsleeves and get down to business. Although it is nearly impossible for a group of board members to collectively turn around a nonprofit, it is critical that those engaged in setting the turnaround strategy keep the other board members involved.

As with staff, board members of the *turnaround* nonprofit will need to be asked to recommit themselves and their energy to the proposed plan of action. In some cases, board members will choose to retreat from the organization at this point due to differences of opinion or lack of time to play a vital role. Departure under these circumstances should be welcomed by those leading the *turnaround* and not seen as failure or lack of commitment.

It is usually a financial crisis that urges a nonprofit to take the *turnaround* route. And by the time this crisis hits, the organization is often mired in past-due payables, current obligations, and without cash. Since it is much easier to get into financial trouble then it is to get out, making the decision to turn around sooner rather than later is to a nonprofit's advantage. But no matter at what point turnaround occurs, serious attention to cash management is nearly always indicated.

Organizations in the *turnaround stage* are willing to take a long and hard look at what's wrong, and irrespective of personal feelings or comfort, to take whatever action is appropriate to reposition the agency according to the needs of the community. (See Chapter 9 for a case illustration)

Effectively managed, turnaround brings an organization back to the high side of the start-up or early growth stage with smaller programs, staff, and budgets but with stronger, flexible, and more relevant mission and services.

CHALLENGES OF THE TURNAROUND STAGE
- Finding a turnaround champion and letting him or her lead

- Establishing a turnaround culture and mindset

- Committing to a consistently frank and open dialogue with constituents, funders, and the community

- Cutting expenditures to reflect realistic income

- Restoring eroded community credibility through consistency, honesty, and results

The Terminal Stage: In Name Only
The stage when an organization has neither the purpose, the will, nor the energy to continue.

At the far end of the lifecycle curve is the *terminal stage,* the stage that occurs when nonprofits, for whatever reason, lose their organizational purpose, will, or energy to stay alive.

Not all *terminal stage* nonprofits look alike. The easy ones to spot are those that have shut down operations, or that continue to exist in name only. Yet some nonprofits make a deliberate and strategic decision to become *terminal* after a pre-ordained number of years or having accomplished their given purpose. In other words, they make strategic decisions to become limited-life rather than permanent organizations.

Although the entry into the *terminal stage* from either of these vantage points is quite different, nonprofits in this final stage share something in common: they no longer have all of the five ingredients essential to organizational livelihood. These five ingredients are:

- A *mission* that provides the contextual purpose within which services are defined and results measured

- A *market* of people who need and want their services

- *Management* ~ the right staff, board members or volunteers willing to hold themselves responsible for the program's success and vitality

- Sufficient *money* to support and sustain the organization going forward, and

- *Energy* ~ the enthusiasm and positive spirit it takes to continually nourish programs and encourage board, staff, and constituents.

THE DECLINE TO TERMINAL PROGRESSION
By the time nonprofits enter the *terminal stage* from *decline,* they have generally been through years of organizational paralysis, and are most likely

stuck in the proverbial rut with no perceived way out. Many are still committed to a mission, but the manifestations of that mission ~ program and services ~ are often no longer relevant to the community. These groups become a metaphor for the old Neil Diamond song *"I am, I said, to no one there."* If programs continue to exist they may be sporadic, unreliable, and undependable.

Board and staff in the *decline* to *terminal stage* have often lost their drive to continue. They look to others for their own spark and often give over their responsibility for sustenance and maintenance of the nonprofit to an outside funder, consultant, or other third party. In some cases, especially where much has been invested or where no other service exists, outside funders or consultants will be tempted to inject cash or expertise to hold the organization together. However (and funders take note), if *internal energy* doesn't exist, any efforts from well-intentioned outsiders will just prolong the *terminal* period. (For more on this subject, see *Chapter 9: Effecting a Turnaround*)

Decline to *terminal* nonprofits are usually deficit spending or using restricted or endowment funds for general operations. In many ways, money is the most fixable problem in a *terminal* nonprofit. And, if lack of money is the only problem the organization has, it should be able to turnaround. Money generally attaches itself to organizations with vital missions, strong community need, responsible staff and management, and energy. So of all the problems a *terminal* nonprofit has, money is usually the least of them.

In the *terminal stage,* systems become unused and maybe even irrelevant. Many *terminal* organizations don't even open their mail. Nor do they return phone calls or reconcile bank statements. In a sense, they are in an organizational depression and behave as if they can escape the reality if they just don't know what's going on.

In fact, many *decline* to *terminal* nonprofits fail to recognize that they are terminal. They somehow manage to function in a marginalized capacity for a long time before taking steps toward renewal or calling it quits. Indeed, some *decline* to *terminal* nonprofits never formally close up shop. They just wither away.

THE *STRATEGICALLY TERMINAL* NONPROFIT

Although equally "terminal," when nonprofits make a conscious choice to go out of business, they generally do so deliberately with eyes wide open, and with a positive sense of accomplishment. Their proactive decisions, though, don't preclude an accompanying sense of loss. In fact, most nonprofits that choose to close, even under the best of circumstances, experience a grieving process even as they work positively to bring the organization to closure.

Nonprofit boards decide to become "limited life" rather than permanent corporations for several reasons. Sometimes a founding gift restricts the organization to a certain number of years. I worked once with an organization whose sole source of funds was a very large sum of money meant to fund a designated number of scholarships. A sunset year was established at the outset by which all the scholarships would be awarded and, when that year occurred, the organization took steps to go out of business in an orderly fashion.

There are other examples from the arts world where, upon the retirement of an artistic founder, the board and founder mutually decide to disband the entity rather than continue. One such example is the *Dale Warland Singers,* a preeminent choral ensemble dedicated to world-class performance of a capella choral music. According to the managing director, when the chorus' namesake founder and well-known artistic director unexpectedly announced his decision to retire at the end of the 2003-2004 season, "our entire focus changed from one of growing an organization to figuring out how to close with dignity and integrity." (For more about the legacy of the Dale Warland Singers see www.dalewarlandsingers.org)

In both these cases, the organizations' boards played an active role in making the decision to dissolve their corporations. Here is another place where the *strategically terminal* nonprofit differs from the *decline* to *terminal* one. The strategically terminal board is active and present. Board members conduct appropriate due diligence after which they make an informed decision to exercise the option of institutional termination. From this decision, staff then carries out the necessary legal and financial decisions to make sure the organization goes out of business with respect and dignity.

CHALLENGES OF THE TERMINAL STAGE
- Accepting responsibility for the organization's renewal or termination

- Resisting the urge to blame others for the terminal situation

- Communicating termination plans to clients with appropriate referrals

- Closing up shop in an honorable manner

LIFECYCLE CHALLENGES

Stage 1: Idea
- Identifying an unmet need
- Developing mission and vision
- Mobilizing the support of others
- Converting an idea into action

Stage 2: Start-up
- Sharing vision and organizational responsibility with staff, board, and constituents
- Knowing when to say "no"
- Hiring versatile staff
- Leveraging sweat equity into outside support
- Living within financial means

Stage 3: Growth
- Too much to do, too little time
- Developing board ownership
- Creating a strategic focus that does not trap creativity and vision
- Developing and identifying distinctive competence
- Beginning to formalize organizational structure
- Becoming comfortable with change
- Diversifying revenues and managing cash flow

Stage 4: Maturity
- Remaining client centered rather than policy bound
- Keeping staff motivated around mission
- Building financial footings of endowments or reserves
- Maintaining a program "edge" of relevance and vibrancy
- Becoming position rather than person dependent

Stage 5: Decline
- Reconnecting with community need, discarding duplicative programs that add no value
- Remembering that policies, procedures, systems, and structure are no substitute for creativity and risk taking
- Keeping board informed and engaged
- Raising enough operating income so reserves are not drawn down for everyday use
- Examining the budget for top-heavy administrative expenses

Stage 6: Turnaround
- Finding a turnaround champion and letting him or her lead
- Establishing a turnaround culture and mindset
- Committing to a consistently frank and open dialogue with constituents, funders, and the community
- Cutting expenditures to reflect realistic income
- Restoring eroded community credibility through consistency, honesty, and program results

Stage 7: Terminal
- Accepting responsibility for organizational renewal or termination
- Resisting the urge to blame others for terminal situation
- Communicating termination plans to clients and making appropriate referrals
- Closing up shop in an honorable manner, worthy of the care in which the nonprofit was founded

4

DIAGNOSING
NONPROFIT CAPACITY

*I have an existential map. It has 'you are here' written
all over it.*

Steven Wright

Although some may use lifecycle theory to explain organizational growth
and development, from a practitioner's standpoint, its most important
contribution is as a *diagnostic tool* for defining the "normal" characteristics
and predictive challenges organizations face at each life stage.[xviii] The stage-
based descriptions, characteristics and performance outcomes found in
this and the previous chapters underscore a fundamental lifecycle premise:
*the challenges and tasks nonprofits face on the way to maturity will be differ-
ent depending on their respective stages of development.*

    This chapter puts the lifecycle definitions into a diagnostic framework.
Using the *Nonprofit Lifecycles Reference Guide* found at the end of this chapter, it introduces a further elaboration of the simple lifecycle diagnostic
developmental curve and demonstrates how to pinpoint specific areas of
capacity weakness and target opportunities for improvement according to
each developmental stage.

Lifecycle Theory as a Diagnostic Framework

Lifecycle diagnosis bridges theory and practice by responding practically to
a particular organization's distinctive developmental issues within the context of the challenges "normal" to that lifecycle stage. In the Introduction
to this book, I referenced my preference for the word diagnosis, rather than
assessment or evaluation. The concept of *diagnosis* is systematic, targeted,
and strategic. It pinpoints both the problem and the solution, thus ensuring accurate assumptions about what's wrong and conclusions about what
to do about it. This has enormous practical and financial consequences for

Capacity-building programs
that don't start with
lifecycle diagnosis run the
risk of assuming all organizations are starting from
the same place. Worse
yet, if they offer one-size
solutions as their methods,
nonprofits may have to
leap-frog over important
developmental tasks
foundational to capacity
building. Applying the
wrong techniques to a misdiagnosed organizational
problem wastes precious
resources and time.
Worse yet, it can add to
an organization's problems,
and exacerbate a
general sense of failure
rather than improvement.

nonprofits and their funders concerned with getting the solution right the first time.

Capacity-building programs that don't start with lifecycle diagnosis run the risk of assuming all organizations are starting from the same place. Worse yet, if they offer one-size solutions as their methods, nonprofits may have to leap-frog over important developmental tasks foundational to capacity building. For example, many capacity-building programs employ a strategic planning process as their primary capacity-building method. Strategic plans are important instruments for achieving organizational focus and direction, and thus are ideal instruments for the *growth* and *mature* stages. They are not necessarily helpful, though, for *start-up* organizations that don't have enough breadth of programming or experience yet to know on what activities or direction they should focus.

Applying the wrong techniques to a misdiagnosed problem wastes precious resources and time. Worse yet, it can add to an organization's problems and exacerbate a general sense of failure rather than improvement.

Traditionally, organizational development consultants have used the concept of diagnosis to identify which types of consultant and managerial interventions would most likely yield desired improvements. Framing diagnosis and accompanying organizational improvements within a lifecycle framework has the advantage of focusing specifically on the organization at hand, mindful both of the distinctive developmental requirements typical of that stage and how those capacity requirements may shift as the organization continues to develop or move backwards.

Figure 5: Nonprofit Lifecycle Capacity Placement

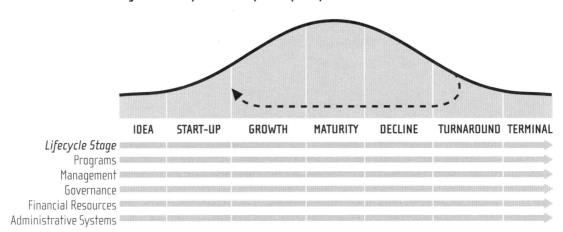

Diagnosing Capacity

Chapter 3 presented a lifecycle framework for diagnostically placing non-profit organizations into one of seven lifecycle stages. As mentioned earlier, some organizations will move backward or forward from their current stage; others, particularly without intervention, will just stay put.

The overall importance of the diagnostic framework is not to worry about movement and improvement until the starting lifecycle point is fully determined. Then the lifecycle model can be taken a step further to pinpoint corresponding capacity requirements one might expect to find at each developmental stage.

Figure 5 shows an expanded lifecycle diagnostic curve, this time with five specific capacity builders applicable to each stage ~ programs, management, board of directors, financial resources, and administrative systems.

These five capacity-building components work together to create the type of predictable tasks and challenges most organizations face at each stage of their development. For the most part, moving from one phase to another requires mastering the challenges attendant to each stage.

Chapter 3 laid out the stage-based description for each of the seven lifecycle stages. The *Nonprofit Lifecycles Reference Guide* at the end of this chapter breaks down those descriptive stages into specific and practical *diagnostic characteristics and performance outcomes* for each of the stages.

To use the lifecycle model as a diagnostic indicator of nonprofit capacity, first refer to the *Nonprofit Lifecycles Reference Guide,* or stage-based descriptions in the preceding chapter, to identify a nonprofit's overall lifecycle position. Then pinpoint the organization's capacity-building diagnosis and opportunities using the following six questions:

- At what overall lifecycle stage is the organization?

- At what stage are its programs? Typically, a nonprofit's programs are far superior to its other infrastructure components.

- Does the current executive director have the right characteristics to lead the organization through this stage of development?

- Is the board assuming roles and responsibilities consistent with the requirements of the life stage?

- Are the financial resources of the organization consistent with those required for that stage of maturation?

- Are current financial and administrative systems in line with the organization's programs and life stage?

One explanation for the high rate of failure of change efforts is that managers and consultants alike frequently fail to diagnose the needs of the organization and to examine feasible routes to change. Instead they implement fashionable administrative techniques and new organization designs without carefully considering whether these tools will help them solve pressing problems and meet the challenges at hand. Nor do they consider whether proposed interventions fit the focal organization. Too often, standard change techniques are good for solving problems other than the ones confronting the organization. Or the tools may be useful for other organizations but not the one needing help now. (*Organizational Diagnosis and Assessment.* Harrison and Shiron, 1999[xix])

Balancing Capacity at Each Lifecycle Stage

The challenge at each lifecycle stage is to achieve complete balance and alignment among a nonprofit's programs, management, governance, resources, and systems.

Figure 6 shows what it looks like to be vertically "in sync" on the lifecycle curve. In this example the nonprofit is functioning nearly completely within the expectations of capacity for the *growth stage.* This does not mean there aren't growing pains or continued challenges. Rather, it means that the likelihood of positive maturation from one developmental stage to the next will be greater since the organization has brought all of its capacity-building requirements into alignment.

Figure 6: Nonprofit Capacity in Alignment

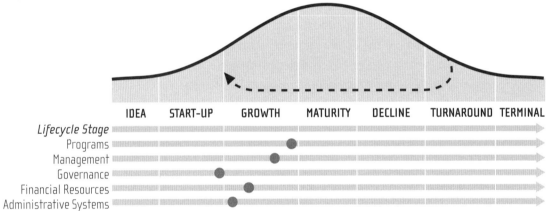

Figure 7: Nonprofit Capacity out of Alignment

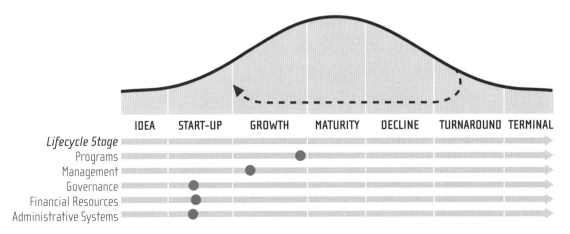

Achieving Lifecycle Capacity

Nonprofits whose management, board, resources, or systems are <u>not</u> functioning at the same level as its programs will find themselves out of sync, or alignment, with the capacity requirements of their lifecycle stage. (See Figure 7) The further behind the lagging point, the more likely that this trouble point will compete with the nonprofit's mission and programs for attention, thus holding the organization back from both capacity and its greater purpose.

Organizations are dynamic entities that cannot be defined precisely by any one model or combination of models. Likewise, some organizations will pre-work or post-work issues at each developmental stage. Thus some *growth-stage* organizations find themselves with administrative systems that are more appropriate to the *start-up* phase, while at the same time, possessing a board of directors which is already functioning at the *mature* level. This is normal since the boundaries between each stage are porous and movement from one stage to the next, although assuming congruence, does not happen in one wholesale leap. (See Highbridge Community Life Center example in Chapter 10)

Applying Lifecycle Diagnosis to Multiple Programs, Affiliates and Strategic Alliances

I am frequently asked by affiliates of national organizations and by executives running large, multi-service agencies if it's possible for various programs within one organization to be at different lifecycle stages. Of course, the answer is yes! Not only can multiple programs or affiliates be in different stages, they most certainly will be.

It is actually in these multiplicitous, complex structures that the lifecycle approach to capacity truly shines. Much like the "Meyers Briggs," the language of lifecycles provides a neutral, non-judgmental framework for staff and management to understand each program's similarities and differences. Once a sub-program's starting-point is understood and accepted, appropriate capacity expectations can be set and agreed upon. The insight and buy-in achieved by this stage-based approach ends up providing a much more solid set of capacity expectations than one-sized platitudes about how all nonprofit programs, whether *start-up* or *mature*, "should" function.

The lifecycle application to mergers or strategic alliances is equally relatable. Through the years, as I have worked with nonprofits seeking to merge or develop strategic alliances, once the mission synergy is agreed upon, one of the first things I look at is each partner's lifecycle stage.

Invariably, many of the conflicts (large or small) that occur as a merger gets underway come from differing expectations. More often than not, the expectation disconnects would have been avoided if the lifecycle stage of each party had been taken into consideration. The more out-of-sync the life stage of each partner, the more time must be spent setting appropriate and achievable expectations. Lifecycle diagnostics and language helps each partner "keep it real" in these situations.

Summary

The seminal tenets of lifecycle theory mentioned earlier in this book are worth summarizing again here.

- *There can be no definition of nonprofit capacity without a stage-based approach.* Capacity will look different from one stage to another.

- *The lifecycle model is diagnostic, not deterministic.* It is meant to identify an organization's capacity starting point, and, by virtue of the placement, understand the dynamic stage-related challenges organizations will face at that stage of development.

- *The lifecycle model is not necessarily sequential or evolutionary.* Not all organizations go through all stages, nor, if they do move from one stage to another, is the movement sequential or progressive. Many organizations move directly from *start-up* to *terminal*. Others, despite thirty years in business, never leave the *start-up* stage.

- *The nonprofit lifecycle model is not age or size dependent.* Rather, it assumes that there are a series of predictable tasks to be accomplished at each of seven discrete stages, along with a set of stage-appropriate expectations to be fulfilled.

- *The lifecycle model is holistic.* It assumes there are multiple infrastructure requirements necessary to manage, govern, fund, and build durable systems in support of a nonprofit's programs. These infrastructural requirements, or *capacity builders*, give specific texture and form to each of the seven stages. They work together to create the multiple, complex, but predictable tasks and outcomes every nonprofit must face and master at each stage of operations.

- *It is a long way from start-up to maturity and there are few, if any, shortcuts.* It is also an expensive road particularly in the *growth-stage* when capacity development usually begins in earnest.

- *The more advanced an organization is in its lifecycle development, the more that can be expected of it.* Thus grantmakers, board members, and even staff should be able to have higher expectations of a *mature* organization than they would of a *start-up.*

- *The lifecycle challenge is to achieve balance or complete alignment among programs, management, governance, resources, and systems at each stage.* Until balance is reached, the "stalled" capacity point will continually hold the organization back. Efforts to press on with mission or new programs will wobble, generally not because of missed market demand or opportunity, but because of structural management, governance, financial, or system weaknesses.

With this framework in mind, let us now look at the diagnostic characteristics of the seven lifecycle stages, along with the respective performance outcomes required to successfully move to the next stage.

Figure 5: Nonprofit Lifecycle Capacity Placement

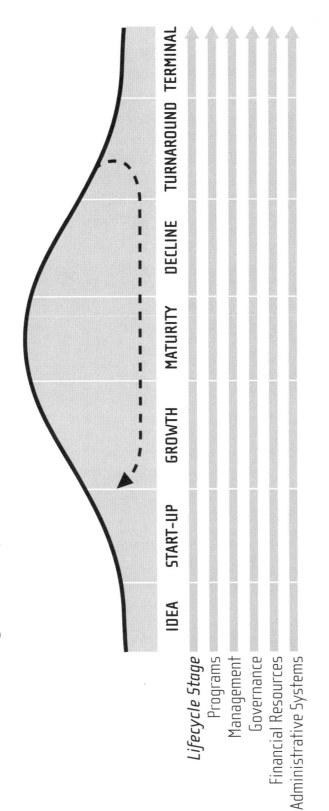

NONPROFIT LIFECYCLES REFERENCE GUIDE

THE IDEA STAGE

	Diagnostic Characteristics	Performance Outcomes
Overview	Perceived community need sparks a founding idea or vision of what could be	A new program or nonprofit corporation is created and tax-exempt status secured
Programs	Programs are not yet defined, only the intense, personal mandate to fill a societal gap	There is clarity of purpose about why the venture is being formed and who will benefit
Management	Originators are believable, action-oriented people with commitment to proposed purpose	Originators are committed to serving as volunteers until resources can be obtained and paid staff recruited
Governance	No board exists at this stage, only supporters with a personal connection to mission	A board has been formed, by-laws developed, and articles of incorporation filed
Resources	Sweat equity is the usual self-funding device, unless originators have deep pockets or an outside "angel" backs the project	Organization begins to convince others with financial resources to support mission
Systems	Although generally lacking in systems, in-kind services, equipment, and other goods may exist	Systems are in place to track donations, income, and disbursements

THE START-UP STAGE

	Diagnostic Characteristics	Performance Outcomes
Overview	The beginning stage of operations when energy and passion are at their highest, but systems generally lag far behind	Organization has proven that its services can and should exist and has established community demand for its programs
Programs	Programs are simple, experimental, and generally have more breadth than depth	Services are being delivered that meet client needs and expectations
	Willingness to do almost anything to prove that services can and should exist	General services have been differentiated into identifiable programs
	Energy and dedication may take precedence over quality and protocols	Minimal quality standards are set, and nonprofit has learned to say "no" rather than do a poor job
Management	Leader is a "spark-plug" and the group's most experienced staff person	Other staff are invested and share organizational commitment and knowledge
	First staff are generalists, wear multiple hats and live the mission with complete enthusiasm	Staff have specific positions and duties and are committed to building a durable organization as they live the mission
	Managers and staff thrive on the thrill of not knowing what tomorrow will bring	Basic organizational activities have been routinized and roles clarified
Governance	Members almost always have a personal connection to mission or founder	Membership has expanded beyond friends of the founder
	High respect for charisma, self-sacrifice and sweat equity of the founder can cause members to defer rightful board decisions to founder or staff	Members understand that the organization is a nonprofit corporation, not a sole-proprietorship and thus make decisions in the *organization's* best interest
	Board operates as a committee of the whole; members generally do not view themselves in a "governance" role	Enough members are committed so that the board has begun to set direction and organizational ownership no longer resides with staff alone
Resources	Usually a low-budget, bootstrap operation unless seeded initially by a major start-up grant	Organization has attracted more than one source of outside funding
	Budget is often the sole financial document	Nonprofit knows where it stands financially, and lives within its income
	Organization usually operates on a cash rather than accrual basis	Nonprofit has learned to manage cash flow
Systems	Financial and administrative functions and systems are generally weak and may be outsourced to others	Organization has shifted resources once dedicated exclusively to mission delivery to development of basic bookkeeping and administrative systems

THE GROWTH STAGE

	Diagnostic Characteristics	Performance Outcomes
Overview	Program opportunity and service demand exceed current systems and structural capabilities	Organization has recognized the link between successful programming and a strong organizational platform
Programs	Organization begins to understand and define the distinctive methods and approach that separates its programming from others	Organization is known for a distinctive programming approach which distinguishes them from their peers
	Organization begins to find the right service mix, focussing on developing a specific niche to a specific clientele.	Organization begins to operate with a strategic plan that is not opportunity adverse, but, instead, focuses and contains organizational energies
	Services begin to be less person-dependent and more positional	Organization has become less dependent on individuals who created programs and more model-driven
Management	Organization is led by people who see infinite potential for services	Management is willing to balance opportunity with strategy and focus
	Staff battle against lack of time and a general sense of urgency; there is always something more to be done	Organization has developed a flexible focus on organizational priorities, rather than ad hoc decisions
	Staff are exhausted and tired of continual "change"	Formalization of job and role descriptions contains burnout and begins to create a new kind of order
	First introduction of staff specialists who require competitive compensation	Work environment is geared to attracting and retaining quality staff
	Founder (when present) may show ambivalence about changes necessitated by growth	Founder separates personal needs from those of the organization
Governance	Board moves beyond "friends" with personal affiliations and recruits outside professionals who bring increased expectations for performance	Nonprofit transitions from a staff-driven model to one of shared board/staff ownership; members understand their governance roles
	Board members need to be able to understand risk and make informed decisions expeditiously as opportunities arise	Board members regularly attend meetings and are willing to make informed, time-sensitive decisions
	Board structure begins to appear	Committee structure, terms of office, and recruitment processes are established
Resources	More sources of income create greater accounting and compliance complexities	In-house financial expertise now exists including a trained accountant commensurate with organizational needs
	Beginning movement from income-only focus toward concern about balance sheet and asset issues	Income has been diversified and organization has a sense of its economics and financial requirements
	More sophisticated financial tracking systems are required	Regular, timely, and useful financial information is available to the board, management and outside funders
Systems	Current systems, never good to begin with, must now be substantially improved to meet demands of continual program expansion and rising compliance expectations	Administrative, financial, and communication systems have been updated and professionalized to support the expanding and complex program array

THE MATURE STAGE

	Diagnostic Characteristics	Performance Outcomes
Overview	The nonprofit has a reputation for providing steady, relevant and vital services to the community and operates with a solid organizational foundation and an overall sense of security	Organization renews itself by staying market-focused and in touch with community while balancing its programs against strategic plans and competencies
Programs	Programs are well organized, results-focused and in touch with community needs	Nonprofit has strong, solid programs and the ability to analyze external changes that may affect current programming
	Organization balances favorite programs and methods against community relevance	Programs are comprehensive, multi-dimensional, and a mix of new and established
	Nonprofit resists the urge to play it safe and knows how to keep its spark alive through continual program renewal	Competitive advantage is maintained by cycling new programs in to replace those losing market share
Management	Executive leadership is often second or third generation from the originators	Executive director is resilient and anticipatory and takes responsibility for organization's success or failure
	Management is perceived as leader among industry peers	Management participates in field development and public policy
	Staff is seasoned and able to manage delegated functions	Organization has staff "bench strength," and individuals cross trained in other positions
	Executive director inspires confidence in staff, board and community	Work environment attracts and retains high quality, motivated staff connected to mission and community need
Governance	Board sets direction, is policy-oriented and leaves management to executive director	Board operates in a policy mode and understands governance, legal and fiduciary responsibilities
	Board plays a leadership role and has the competence to keep nonprofit focussed and vital	Board has determined how to monitor organizational impact on the community
	Board is organized for maximum effectiveness and has a structure for continuity of leadership and culture	Board committee structure is clearly defined, members appropriately competent and diverse, with rotating terms of office
Resources	Organization has multiple sources of income and is not dependent on one source of funding	A financial backbone of diversified, stable income sources exists
	Accurate financial forecasts are made and deficits generally avoided	Financial systems anticipate and course-correct inaccurate income and cost projections
	Organization has sufficient financial flexibility to at least partially self-fund new initiatives	Nonprofit has ready access to working capital through internal reserves or bank loans
Systems	Administrative systems are at or near level of sophistication required for competent management and decision-making	Systems are continually reassessed for adequacy to keep pace with program and administrative requirements
	Organization operates from an outlined course of action for routine client, board and personnel matters	Client grievance procedures and personnel policies are in place; board manuals and employee handbooks exist
	Regular communication mechanisms exist within the agency and with outside publics	Annual reports and other marketing materials are produced that effectively tell the organization's story

	Diagnostic Characteristics	Performance Outcomes (to positively move out of this stage)
Overview	Organization makes status quo decisions based on internal factors rather than external client needs that result in diminished client census and insufficient current income to cover operating expenses	A board member, staff person, or funder intervenes to force reality-based organizational self-awareness, and leads to full turnaround or regeneration
Programs	Programs are rigid, status quo, method focused, and inordinately focused on pride in past achievements	Organization has brought in new voices, insight, and approaches and is willing to discard programs that duplicate or bring no added value to the community
	Programs are losing clients to others whose approach is more accessible, and possibly less expensive	Program accessibility and cost structures are re-examined from a client-centered approach
	Client feedback mechanisms don't exist, and customer service processes may be cumbersome	A client-oriented, results-based approach has been developed to replace process-orientated systems
Management	Management is complacent and committed to status quo	Nonprofits entrenched in decline generally require new leadership for turnaround to occur
	Organizational slippage is either unseen, denied, or blamed on external sources	Self-awareness is reached about agency's deteriorating condition and commitment to turn it around
	Management is trapped by commitment to programs, staff, systems, or policies, no matter how outdated or poorly they are working	Management adapts quickly to setbacks and changing circumstances, focusing on action and solutions rather than on prior practices
Governance	Board is unaware there is something wrong; they think things are running smoothly and often don't take action until money starts running out	Board regularly requires and reviews client performance information and satisfaction measurements in addition to financial reports
	Lack of organizational "spark," or one too many crises, causes ennui and diminished attendance	Members attend board meetings on a regular basis
	Board may operate with a strategic plan, but it is focused on "what *we* want to do" rather than community need	Board members are future-focussed, not complacent, and serve as program ambassadors, keeping their ears to the ground of community need
	A new board member is generally the "whistle-blower," calling the status quo into question and, if willing, puts the turnaround process in motion	Someone is willing to openly call the board's attention to organizational "slippage" and develop a game plan to correct it
Resources	Organization is adverse to cutting expenses even though declining client census results in decreased revenues and grant support	Budgets are built and maintained based on realistic income projections; expenses are cut in keeping with the realities of current income
	Asset-rich organizations look to the balance sheet's prior earnings to cover current expenses	Current operating income is sufficient to cover annual operating expenses
	Fixed assets may be inflexible to changing program need, and contribute to program decline	All assets are examined in light of current needs and program requirements
	Budgets are fixed-cost and expense heavy, with income projections reflecting past experience rather than current reality	Budgets reflect break-even cost analysis on each program and realistic income projections
Systems	Systems, although developed, are often antiquated, and physical space may be deteriorating	Systems are reviewed in light of changing program dynamics, and attention is paid to cleanliness and repair of physical space

	Diagnostic Characteristics	Performance Outcomes
Overview	An organization that is at a critical juncture because of lost market share and revenues, but, through self-awareness and determination, has taken decisive action to reverse prior actions in favor of market relevance and organizational viability	Organization has restructured its programs, management, finances, and marketing strategies in light of community need, relevance and financial realities
Programs	Programs are reassessed and modified in light of current market needs and financial viability	Programs have been examined for market and mission relevance
	Client, constituent and funder input is sought for program redefinition	Program credibility has been reestablished with constituents
	Programs are probably fewer in number than before	Fewer programs, but more solid and client-focussed
Management	Turnaround leader is a gutsy, strong-willed person with a clear sense of direction and the ability to inspire confidence in others	Management owns past problems (even those they were not there for) and has reestablished community and client confidence
	Manager is decisive, able to size up problems, and mobilizes resources effectively	Management has streamlined personnel and changed organizational structure in light of resource availability
	Management has gained staff buy-in and no longer makes community promises it can't keep	Organization has the capacity to think again about the future knowing it has the staff and constituent support
Governance	A core of committed board members are ready to do what it takes to restore organizational integrity	Board has affirmatively reconnected with the organization and is eager to help restore institutional integrity
	Turnover has shrunk board down to only the committed members	Small but highly committed group takes the organization forward
	Board supports turnaround manager in leadership role and helps to regain institutional credibility	Board provides objectivity, support and advice to turnaround manager
Resources	Financial crisis is the usual trigger-point, which, by the time it is addressed, leaves the organization short or out of cash	Staff and board understand the financial behavior that led to the crisis and are committed to not repeating
	Willingness to cut expenses to reflect realistic income and cash flow	Payment plans consistent with cash flow have been worked out with creditors and are being adhered to
Systems	Existing policies and procedures may be too complex, expensive, and "mature" for the turnaround organization	Policies and procedures have been streamlined and now match the organization's cash position and downsized requirements

	Diagnostic Characteristics	**Performance Outcomes**
Overview	An organization that has lost its will, reason, or energy to exist.	Organization accepts responsibility to cease operations in a manner respectful of its past.
Programs	Programs are unreliable, unsteady, and seriously underfunded	Termination plans are communicated to clients in a professional manner, making appropriate referrals as indicated
Management	Staff and management have dwindled to a handful and possibly may be working without pay	Management communicates plans to funders and other constituents
Governance	Board has lost its collective drive to continue and may exist in name only	Board fulfills its due diligence requirements regarding disposition of assets, closing accounts, and distributing remaining funds to another nonprofit
Resources	The organization is most likely out of money and may have accumulated deficits	A comprehensive analysis of all outstanding debt is completed.
	Creditor calls are persistent and insistent	Organization communicates honestly with creditors, making discounted payment arrangements if necessary and possible
	Funders have stopped multiple-year grants	Restricted grants are returned to funders unless alternative plans have been made
Systems	Systems have been abandoned. Organizational decisions and general workflow happen on an ad hoc basis	Attorney is consulted to ensure federal termination notices have been met and storage arrangements made for records required by the IRS

Part Two : LIFECYCLES IN ACTION

5

LIFECYCLE MANAGEMENT

There are no shortcuts to anyplace worth going.

Beverly Sills

Managing a nonprofit in today's world is a tough task, no matter what your lifecycle stage. Whether it's personnel, money, governance, systems, or space issues, to be "nonprofit" today almost guarantees the need to do more with less, while still in fierce pursuit of mission. It's precisely because you've got neither time nor money to waste that a lifecycle approach to management makes such eminent sense.

This section of *NONPROFIT LIFECYCLES* is written especially for nonprofit managers, board members, and those potentially interested in working in the nonprofit sector. It is organized into five chapters, all concerned with the management and governance challenges nonprofits face on the way to maturity and sustainability. This section begins with an overview chapter, *Lifecycle Management,* which tackles two subjects that overarch each lifecycle stage: human and financial resources. Each subsequent chapter then presents four critical management junctures nonprofits face in various stages of development: *founder transitions, developing board ownership, second-stage management,* and *effecting a turnaround.* Although these aren't the only challenges along the path to capacity and sustainability, in my experience as a management consultant, the challenges presented in the next four chapters represent universally critical moments. If effectively achieved, these junctures help nonprofits progress into higher levels of organizational competency and performance.

Each chapter begins with an overview of the topic, followed by a reality-based (but fictional) case study that illustrates both the topic and overall lifecycle gestalt. In this way, foundation officers and academics may also find this section useful in understanding lifecycle dynamics and how normative challenges play out in nonprofit life.

As with the rest of this book, this section is about promoting insight and understanding, rather than providing answers. It is meant to reinforce how important capacity is to nonprofit mission and program delivery, paint several realistic pictures of capacity challenges in action, and leave you with a better understanding of the management and governance dimensions of capacity at each lifecycle stage.

If you haven't done so already, now would be a good time to go back to Chapter 4 and complete the diagnostic placement of your organization's lifecycle stage. Feel free to copy the *Nonprofit Lifecycle Capacity Placement* diagnostic and to share it with your staff and board members. Some organizations take an entire board meeting to see the extent to which key people agree on the organization's lifecycle placement and corresponding capacity-building needs. This is a really good way to find out if you, your staff, and board are all on the same page. Don't be alarmed if you're not. It's just one more opportunity to understand, communicate, and educate.

Occasionally, nonprofits are afraid to make their capacity challenges explicit to their board or, even more so, to funders. This is another beauty of lifecycle theory. It assumes nonprofits, like any other organizations, have challenges that are all part of the growing up process. Rather than ducking organizational growing pains, the lifecycle approach to capacity treats these challenges as normal and even predictable. Think about it this way. You wouldn't expect a toddler, just learning to walk, to be able to skip across the room. Skipping isn't a "normal" part of a toddler's behavioral repertoire. His school-age sister, on the other hand, should be able to skip without falling. Lifecycle theory establishes similar stage-based expectations for nonprofit capacity.

No matter what the management books say, or how much you wish it wasn't so, your organization is where it is. The only way to move forward or to strengthen your current position, is to embrace honestly your lifecycle stage, fully understand its normative characteristics, and make plans accordingly for self-improvement. It's when nonprofits don't embrace where they are and fully understand their lifecycle capacity requirements that they stall (temporarily or permanently) along the upward side of the curve or fail to reinvigorate themselves if on the downward slope.

We all know organizations that have never made it out of the *start-up* stage. For some, it is an ideological thing. They want to stay "grassroots" and closely connected to their community, neighborhood, or constituency's values. But nothing says those grassroots values can't be maintained

The lifecycle approach to capacity assumes that nonprofits, like any other organization, will have challenges that are all part of the growing up process. Rather than ducking organizational growing pains, the lifecycle approach treats these challenges as normal, and even predictable.

while at the same time strengthening organizational capacity. In fact, the reverse argument could be made. Organizations that operate with capacity are more likely to be able to provide their constituents with the dignity, respect, and resources they deserve.

Second only to *start-up*, the most likely place for nonprofits to stall is the *growth stage*, far and away the most difficult of all the lifecycle stages to manage. By definition, the *growth stage* occurs when a nonprofit's services and programs have now hit the community's radar screen, and folks want whatever it is you are about. This is when the realization begins to hit that you have nowhere near enough internal capacity ~ staff, money, systems, maybe even governance capabilities ~ to take advantage of the opportunities at hand.

Two of the biggest challenge areas where nonprofits generally feel they have the least capacity, at least in their early stages, are human and financial resources. The remainder of this chapter tackles both of these topics from a lifecycle perspective.

Hiring for Lifecycle "Fit"

Anyone who has been in the job world for any length of time has experienced the importance of organizational "fit." Indeed, all too frequently, job applicants find themselves in their dream jobs, perfectly suited to their skills and experience, yet hopelessly out of sync with the culture of the organization itself. Here is yet another application for the lifecycle approach.

I have learned the value of "fit" the hard way, both as an employer and as an employee. Here is one personal example. Several years ago, as the new administrator of a nonprofit agency in the throes of professionalizing its systems and image, I hired a cracker jack secretary, Christine. I was particularly pleased to have recruited someone who had several years previous secretarial experience with a major corporation.

Christine was poised, dressed meticulously, and had the potential to professionalize our written communications while at the same time serve as a role model for our support staff, many of whom could type, but had no previous clerical experience.

Christine began work on August 1, a very hot, humid, Midwestern day. I was secretly pleased that her office was on the garden level of our recently renovated, eighty-year-old building, where it was at least marginally cooler than the rest of the non-air-conditioned space.

The following day, Christine did not come to work. On her desk she had left a note saying it was a "big mistake" to have taken this job. Why? She

> Organizations that operate with capacity are more likely to be able to provide their constituents with the dignity, respect, and resources they deserve.

had assumed certain organizational amenities, like air-conditioning and up-to-date office equipment, which we were clearly without.

I was devastated. For my co-workers and I, who had moved from much more humble quarters, this building, even in the hot summer, was a dream for which we had all worked long and hard. For us, our building was a step-up. For Christine, it was a step (or more) back.

That was my first conscious experience with "fit." Had I realized then that we were a *start-up* agency moving into the *growth stage,* I would not have selected someone who needed a more predictable, stable (and air-conditioned) work setting, or state-of-the-art office equipment, associated with more *mature* organizations. Christine had all the skills and experience I was looking for, but her expectations were completely out of sync with our organization's lifecycle stage. We didn't fit her expectations, and had she stayed, she no doubt would not have fit ours either.

Was Christine wrong for quitting? No. But was there anything "wrong" with our organization? No, again. In fact, this example illustrates another benefit of the lifecycle approach: it can help to depersonalize an otherwise sticky and emotionally charged situation. Looking back on it, I can see where I went wrong in the hiring process. My carefully crafted job descriptions specified only the *professional* requirements of the job: education, experience, and skill. I hadn't considered at all the corresponding *personal* attributes that would allow a candidate to successfully "fit in" to our organizational lifecycle.

Figure 8: Four Criteria for Hiring

Professional requirements ~ education, experience, and skill ~ are the fundamental measurements of any hiring decision. And, indeed, measurements they are, since each of the three is something a person can gain or improve, given time and effort. Both employer and employee, however, pay a price when an individual must struggle to "fit in" to lifecycle stages or cultures inconsistent with their temperament (or values). This struggle usually doesn't happen without the employee having to give up too much of who they are.

As an employer, fit problems are at least partially avoided by first understanding your organization's lifecycle stage and then identifying the type of person most likely to succeed given the realities of temperament and life stage. As an employee, the better you understand your personal attributes, the more able you will be to match them to those likely required by the job's lifecycle stage. Remember too, that many larger organizations have several lifecycles going on at once. It's possible that you are being hired into a *start-up* unit within a *mature* organization.

By the way, everything about the importance of employee "fit" applies to board members too. Some board members are more suited to govern *mature* organizations than *start-ups*, and the other way around. All too often, a person is recruited to what appears to be a *mature* organization's board, only to find out that the organization is actually in *decline.* Although talented board members willing to blow the whistle are exactly what a *decline* board needs, this situation is often more than the incoming board member bargained for. So once again, matching your organization's lifecycle stage with both employee and board member fit will save you and them the angst that invariably follows a poor fit.

The following stage-related attributes may be helpful to nonprofit employers, as well as present or future employees, in determining the personal qualities generally required for each lifecycle stage. This is not meant to be an exhaustive nor prescriptive listing, but rather a set of attributes to get you thinking about potential lifecycle fit.

Lifecycle Management and Leadership Attributes

IDEA STAGE

- Creative
- Free-thinker
- Opportunity-driven
- Not bound by time
- Good understanding of the marketplace
- Single-minded
- Committed to the cause
- Able to follow through

START-UP STAGE

- Energetic
- Able to balance multiple priorities
- Able to handle continual interruptions
- Multi-talented generalist

- Single-minded but adaptable
- Risk-taker

GROWTH STAGE
- Dynamic
- Strong base of personal reserves
- Able to inspire and motivate
- Energetic
- Able to create a plan and provide focus, but veer from it as necessary
- Able to appreciate, create and routinize systems to make certain functions easier
- Good judgment and instinct to know what opportunities to pursue and which to decline
- Comfortable with continual change
- Understand the servant/leader management model

MATURITY STAGE
- Good manager who likes to manage people and processes
- Respected in the field
- Policy and procedures oriented
- Sees the value in stability, while always seeking ways to improve client/community service
- Capable of motivating staff
- Understands and values organizational structure

DECLINE/REGENERATION STAGE
- Committed to mission
- Willingness to shake the status quo
- Capable of objective rather than subjective analysis
- Understands the dynamics of organizational renewal
- Highly responsible with no tendencies to blame or deny
- Able to motivate and lead others to change the status quo

TURNAROUND STAGE
- "Take charge" personality
- Confidence builder
- Highly energetic
- Comfortable with bad news, confrontation, and conflict
- Doesn't take things personally
- Natural problem solver
- Able to make quick decisions, but also capable of long-term thinking
- Doesn't need others' approval

Professional requirements ~ education, experience, and skill ~ are the fundamental measurement of any hiring decision. And, indeed, measurements they are, since each of the three is something a person can gain or improve, given time and effort. Both employer and employee, however, pay a price when an individual must struggle to "fit in" to lifecycle stages or cultures inconsistent with their temperament (or values). This struggle usually doesn't happen without the employee having to give up too much of who they are.

TERMINAL STAGE
- Good communicator
- Able to accomplish tasks in an orderly fashion
- Good negotiator
- Cares about what will happen to clients if organization terminates
- Respectful of process, but capable of some emotional distance

Growing with the Job

Once they've found a good fit, can employees grow with the job? That answer generally depends on the individual's own ability to adapt to the personal qualities required in the new stage of development, along with the specific skills required by the advanced stage.

Growing with the job between the *idea* and *start-up stages* is nearly always possible, since many of the personal qualities required by the stages are similar. Likewise, the personal attributes needed to advance from *start-up* into the early stages of *growth* are also usually transferable. Where managers, and even staff, most frequently feel the pinch is in the following stage transitions:

- The transition between the early stages of *growth* and the later stages of the same period, particularly when growth is rapid and turbulent. The skills needed to focus, strategize, and in some ways "contain" organizational opportunities are frequently out of sync with the natural "builder" inclinations of the *start-up* entrepreneur or those staff who value smaller organizations.

- The transition between *growth* and *maturity*. Maturity requires the ability to get things done through other people and to institutionalize an organizational approach. Frequently the *growth-stage* manager, even those who'd give their eyeteeth for systems, has neither the skill nor experience to implement necessary infrastructural capabilities.

- The transition between *decline* and *turnaround*. Although those at the helm in *decline* can often bring about regeneration, experience indicates that it is next to impossible for those same managers to orchestrate a *turnaround*.

You'll find more examples of lifecycle hiring challenges in the next four chapters. But before moving on to them, let's look at nonprofit lifecycles from a financial perspective.

Just as you would be surprised to find a college student saving for retirement, so too, nonprofits have different financial needs, goals, and challenges at various lifecycle stages.

Lifecycle Financial Goals

Nonprofit managers in late *growth*, *maturity*, and *decline* often tell me it's a toss up as to which is the more continual challenge, people or money. For nonprofits in *start-up* or *early growth* years, there is no contest. The challenge is all about money, and more specifically, how and where to get it.

Mission may be every nonprofit's *raison d'être*, but money is its lifeblood. Despite the wealth of volunteer hours and goods that so generously pervade the nonprofit sector, it still takes money to deliver both social and cultural programs with the quality and consistency demanded by today's society.

Yet money has always been in short supply for the nonprofit sector, so much so, that one of the questions I am asked most frequently is: *How can we establish an endowment?* Depending on the lifecycle stage of the questioner, what they are really asking is, *How can we generate an extra $10,000 or $20,000 for our annual operating budget?* Faced with the definition of endowment ~ a permanent investment, contributed by an outside donor, whose earnings alone are available for annual operations ~ most nonprofits quickly concede that it's not an endowment they want after all, but rather, extra, unrestricted, cash.

Although not appropriate for every nonprofit, endowments illustrate how nonprofit financial goals also follow a lifecycle pattern. Just as you'd be surprised to find a college student saving for retirement, so too, nonprofits have different financial needs, goals, and challenges at various lifecycle stages.

Start-up nonprofits are generally income-focused; it's tough to save money when you are trying to make ends meet. *Growth-stage* nonprofits need cash reserves to stem their cash flow and receivables problems. *Mature* nonprofits are more frequently able to invest funds for a larger period of time, and for some, endowments are just what's needed to perpetuate their services over the long term.

Here is another listing of the typical financial challenges nonprofits are likely to encounter at each lifecycle stage. You might find you've already mastered all the tasks in your particular stage, and are well into pre-working those of the next stage. Maybe too, you'll see you've skipped a step or two as you've raced ahead developmentally. It's never too late to catch up!

Lifecycle Financial Tasks and Challenges

IDEA STAGE

• Obtain funding or financing
• Establish a checking or saving account separate from personal accounts

- Track both income and expense, including personal funds provided to the new venture
- Obtain in-kind services

START-UP STAGE
- Leverage sweat equity into outside support
- Obtain start-up grants or contracts
- Create a break-even budget
- Set up bookkeeping systems to track income and expenses
- Manage cash flow

GROWTH STAGE
- Develop more sophisticated financial statements and begin to manage from them
- Make monthly cash flow forecasts
- Diversify program revenues
- Obtain line of credit or working capital loan to even out cash flow
- Recognize that each program has different costs; some will produce surpluses, some not
- Plan reasonable surpluses into as many programs as possible
- Thoroughly understand and budget administrative costs
- Begin to budget depreciation as an operating expense
- Set aside cash surpluses for working capital reserves

MATURITY STAGE
- Develop net asset balances (equity)
- Create operating reserves from unrestricted income
- Begin or continue to develop working capital reserves to internally finance cash flow and growth
- Set up "repair and replacement" reserves, funded by depreciation allowances
- Possibly develop an endowment, take on a mortgage, or consider other forms of permanent capital

DECLINE STAGE
- Match current income to current expense
- Resist the urge to dip into reserves to cover declining operating income
- Engage in income-based (rather than budget-based) spending[xx]
- Use reserves only for regenerating activities, not for deficit spending
- Examine the budget for top-heavy administrative expenses

TURNAROUND STAGE

- Communicate honestly with creditors, make discounted payments if possible
- Create a financial plan to pay off creditors and restore organizational credibility
- Use cash flow forecasts in addition to other financial statements to balance cash requirements with projected financial receipts
- Consider and obtain a debt consolidation loan to allow you to focus on the future while responsibly handling past debts
- Cut back to minimal expense levels to be sure to stay within organizational means and not exacerbate the financial turnaround problem
- Make sure program managers understand the relationship between budget and cash; just because it's in the budget, doesn't mean there is cash available

TERMINAL STAGE

- Establish an orderly way to go out of business
- Transfer assets to another nonprofit
- Seek legal help!

6

THE FOUNDER'S
LIFECYCLE

Of you who have built castles in the air, your work need not be lost; this is where they should be. Now put the foundations under them.

Henry David Thoreau

It is almost impossible to discuss nonprofit lifecycles, particularly the earlier stages, without considering the critical role of the nonprofit founder in the organization's inception, development, and ultimate maturation.

To understand a founder is to acknowledge right off the bat his or her central role as the organization's originator. No matter how many years since the organization's conception, founders have the same fundamental motivation today they had in the beginning. And for the nonprofit founder, that motivation is generally linked to some hole in the social or cultural status quo that desperately needs to be filled. Yes, desperately. This is another thing to know about founders. They operate from a perceived imperative that has *their* name written in big bold letters.

Nonprofit founders have a calling, a mission, an internal mandate, fueled by classic entrepreneurial characteristics: energy, drive, intensity, self-determination, and urgency. No matter how short or long their tenure, founders are, forever, inextricably linked to their founding organizations. At first this connection is almost synonymous with who they are. Later, as time goes on, the relationship becomes more like a parent with a child. And always, there is pride of ownership. Pride and purpose reign supreme, particularly in the early years.

Founders, like many entrepreneurs, march to their own drummers. They need no one's approval. They defy conventional methods. They know how something must be done, even though they can't tell you how to do it. They believe in themselves and in whatever they are working on at the present moment. They are usually never satisfied. There is always more to be done and never enough time or money to do it.

Like other entrepreneurs, founders are products of their times. The way they manage their organizations and the values they bring to it are frequently rooted in the events of their era, or are a reflection of their own generation. Consequently, organizations founded in the '60s are likely to have a different value-base and mindset than those founded in the '80s, '90s or 2000s.

Founders are also products of their families and upbringing. Through the years several studies have postulated various linkages between the development of an entrepreneurial personality and families of origin. Three family-related theories seem most likely to account for the nonprofit entrepreneurial impulse: an early orientation to achieve, encouraged independence, and/or early need to control their environment. Though most of the research focuses on these as independent variables, in my experience, they are not necessarily mutually exclusive.

> *Achievement-oriented* founders were generally raised in nurturing home environments where they were consistently encouraged and rewarded for achieving. They grew up believing nothing is beyond them.

> *Independence-oriented* founders tend to come from homes where one or both parents were self-employed, providing the child (often the oldest) both a role model of independence as well as early family responsibilities.

> *Control-oriented* founders may have come from families filled with poverty and/or emotional insecurity. Consequently, they needed to grow up fast and take control of their environment since no one was taking care of it for them. Control becomes their security. They grow up believing in themselves and needing to stay in control, particularly when they are threatened or their environment gets hostile.

In consulting situations, when faced with seemingly irrational founder behavior, I have discovered that one of these family of origin theories often provides the key to unlocking the founder's otherwise closed door.

Founders are also frequently leaders, although some fail to lead their own organizations. Like other entrepreneurs, founders generally find management tasks boring and only tolerable as a way to get things organized around them. In fact, founders, at least at the outset, may disdain management. Their energies are absorbed elsewhere. They are driven by the higher goals of mission and purpose. Their job is to create. The task of manage-

The drive for sustainability forces founders to face the toughest of all questions: Do I want my organization to survive me? If so, what must happen to institutionalize my vision?

ment is quite different. It is to organize, systematize, and develop a stable framework for getting the work done and sustaining the organization over time.

The drive for sustainability forces founders to face the toughest of all questions: *Do I want my organization to survive me?* Believe it or not, this question preoccupies most founders, particularly those reaching a certain age. Yet, too often, this question never gets discussed both because founders are often reluctant to bring it up and because board members feel they don't have the right to raise it.

The most strategic question a founder-led organization must ask is whether it is bound for permanence or, instead, is limited to the founder's tenure. Coming to grips with this question sets the backdrop for every subsequent organizational decision. The very process of determining whether the organization should succeed its founder often requires facing a founder's *ungoverned ownership*, which studies consistently identify as one of the major roadblocks to perpetuating an organization beyond its founder.

Three Stages of Founder Separation

If permanence is an organizational goal, founders can expect three stages of separation in the transition from being "the one" to being "one of." Each paves the way for institutional sustainability.

Delegation

The first stage is *delegation*. As the founder's fledgling organization begins to achieve success, four shows in a ninety-nine seat theater are not enough. The calling is much greater than this. But more shows (or, for social services, more programs) mean more money, more staff, and more attention to management and administrative systems. All of this takes the founder's focus off creativity and "down" to business.

At this point, a founder has two choices: to continue to proceed solo or to hire a manager to head up the business side of the operation. This decision is generally a no-brainer, since the founder was born to lead, not to manage. So a business manager (a.k.a. a managing director, general manager, or executive director) is hired.

The delegation phase of separation begins when founders decide they can't do it all themselves. They need help. Yet, even if a founder masters the art of delegation (and many don't), the founder remains the indisputable leader of the organization at this point. He or she may now have a new manager, but no matter what the title or job description may say or what the board may intend, in the founder's eyes the new hire is there for one, and only one, reason ~ to help the founder. At this stage, the founder is still in the driver's seat. Any management person (and all too often the board as well) is merely riding shotgun.

Hiring its first professional staff is one of the most difficult tasks any young organization faces, whether founder-led or not. A combination of hiring inexperience on the part of the founder and the board, and the need for a can-do generalist, makes it easy to miss the mark the first or second time around. Couple that with low wages, and the founder's often unrealistic expectations that the new hire will "give all" just like he or she does, and you can see why it takes such a long time and so many misses for founders and boards to successfully recruit and maintain a competent team of professionals.

Separate Identities

The next stage of separation, *individuation*, occurs (and it can be years later or never at all) when the founder begins to think of the organization as separate from him or herself. This is a profound moment in a founder's life that results in a psychic separation of his or her personal identity and goals from his or her role as a founder. This can be, and frequently is, a real identity crisis, but one that must be mastered for institutionalization beyond the founder to occur.

The impetus to separate the two identities may be personal (a milestone birthday, becoming an empty nester, or some other soul-searching event). It may occur as a result of rapid growth or a major organizational challenge, or the founder may have just grown tired of the burden of sole psychic ownership. Whatever the case, it hits like a ton of bricks: *My creation is bigger than I am.* It has a life of its own. The organization that once depended on the founder for every creative idea and decision, and upon whom the founder depended for personal identity, is becoming separate and other.

This is among the most critical junctures in any permanent organization's growth and development. It also sets the stage for how successfully and positively founders can continue to be involved in their creations. It is at this point that founders realize that the success of their creation requires true partners, people who are their equal or better. These partners aren't helpmates as in the delegation stage. They are *real* executive, managing, or program directors and *real* boards of directors.

Although the *growth stage* is full of many other critical challenges, when founders are present, the most critical juncture of all is orchestrating this

---

Founders who put their organization's changing needs ahead of their own natural inclinations can generally successfully continue to grow with their developing company. Indeed, successful founders are those who have learned to adapt to their organization's ever-changing lifecycle needs.

second-stage founder separation. In lifecycle theory, we refer to this phenomenon as *transference of sole organizational ownership* from the founder to both the board of directors and to the management counterpart. This transference implies shared ownership and interdependence. The organization no longer belongs just to the founder. The founder's gift has gone public. It is now co-owned by the community represented by the board and staff.

In theory, of course, it was always supposed to be this way. But with founders still active in the organization, transference and interdependence aren't generally possible until the founder has the ton-of-bricks awakening mentioned above. If the founder comes to this understanding on his or her own, the partnership is much more likely to "take" (albeit painfully) than it would as an ultimatum from others. In my experience, when frustrated boards hire managing directors or institute governance ultimatums against the wishes or without the buy-in of the founder, the efforts generally fail. Right idea, wrong set-up.

In the second stage of separation, the founder now has two roles: the position stated in his or her job description, and his or her position as originator. The founder position, of course, can never be taken away. It deserves respect and continued acknowledgement. But the other role, the one on the job description, is another story. That role requires a certain level of performance that moves the organization forward. Here founders can't rest on their laurels. Whatever their role may be, they must provide the leadership, management, or governance required by that role. There can be no hiding behind their other role as founder.

In the second stage of separation, the founder now has two roles: the position stated in his or her job description, and his or her position as originator.

Institutionalization

As painful as identity separation is, the third stage of founder separation, *institutionalization*, requires another psychic leap on the part of the founder. This is an especially tricky separation since building an institution is not only antithetical to a founder's entrepreneurial instincts, but can also be his or her first encounter with personal or professional mortality.

In this phase, the founder, who may now be approaching mid-life, begins to count his or her remaining work years on one or two hands. No matter how youthful and still full of great ideas, the founder knows his or her days are numbered. Now the task is how to make the most of them.

When managed properly, third-stage institutional separation can be a very powerful transition, even a gift, for those who have mastered individuation. It is a chance for founders to step back, and with some distance, define a new role for themselves while ensuring that every function previously performed has now shifted to worthy successors, others who care about the organization.

In the commercial world, this process is called exit or succession planning. But these words have little ring to nonprofit founders who are more intent on transferring their values than on planning for their physical succession ~ and rightly so. For it is a nonprofit founder's values and aspirations that form his or her greatest legacy. Identifying these values and seeding them throughout the organization is a worthwhile and meaningful use of the founder's time and energy at this institutional stage.

Figure 9: Stages of Founder Separation

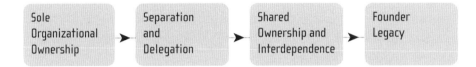

Too often though, founders, by default, end up single-handedly orchestrating their own succession. As much as a founder may want a role in conceptualizing or even choosing his or her successor, this final transition should not be left to the founder alone. The process of facilitating the founder's positive and honorable succession belongs to the board.

Furthermore, in today's rapidly changing world, simply replacing a founder is not always the best method of sustaining an important community institution. Increasingly, we are seeing examples of founder-led organizations and their boards bringing the same creativity to the institutionalization of their organizations that was directed to their initial creation. Rather than opting for the traditional single-person successor, some organizations will place themselves under the umbrella of a larger institution ~ a university, a larger social service agency, or performing arts center. Others will band together with mission-compatible cohorts creating new synergy and renewed impetus. Such non-traditional options may present the best avenue of sustaining an organization whose founder has either left or successfully moved into a staff role.

Three valuable resources conclude this chapter. The first is a *Board Member's Guide to Founder Succession*. Originally published in an article *Helping Founders Succeed,* [xxi] this list was inspired by a retreat I conducted with a group of nonprofit founders, many of whom were also founding influences in their respective fields.

A Board Member's Guide to Founder Succession

- As early in your organization's life as practical, begin open discussion about whether you have a "limited life" corporation or one whose value to society supersedes the person of the founder. Then function accordingly.

- Understand your founder's underlying motivation, both in terms of his or her mission and psyche. Let the achievement-oriented founder achieve. Structure the independent founder's role with enough autonomy and elbow-room that he or she doesn't feel trapped of fenced in. Build security into the control-oriented founder's job. The more secure he or she feels, the less the founder will feel the need to control.

- Surround your founder with competent professional staff and board members, the best you can afford. Founders find it hard enough to give up control. The challenge is even more difficult when the organization can afford only under-skilled staff and managers. Lack of competent, experienced staff and board members can play a significant role in a founder's failure to let go.

- Recruit mission-motivated, retired CEOs to your board, as well as entrepreneurs who have built and sold their businesses or made transitions into new roles within their organizations. Their experience provides a number of benefits to a founder-led organization, not the least of which is their personal experiences with separation or succession.

- Understand that successfully moving beyond a founder will be a two-steps forward, one-step back process. Support the positive efforts, coach through the back-sliding, and remind your founder of the shared goal of permanence.

- Hold your founder accountable for his or her management position. The founder may be a giant in his or her field, but if he or she holds a staff position in the organization, the founder is responsible for performing in a way that strengthens the organization. Offer the founder an emeritus position if he or she can't or chooses not to pull the full weight of his or her staff position.

- Likewise, pull your own weight. Show up, prepared. You are not just a volunteer stakeholder; you hold the ultimate responsibility for governing the organization through its quest for sustainability.

- Encourage your founder's reinvention as a professional. Love of the work he or she set out to do is still at the core of your founder's motivation.

- Encourage your founder to have a personal board of advisors, people who will offer them support and respect and who will give them good solid advice. This is especially important to founders as they maneuver through second and third stage separation. Too many conflicts of interest occur when the organization's board is also the founder's advisors. The board of directors, while respecting the founder's role, needs to make decisions in the best interest of the organization.

- Encourage a systematic process for your founder to transfer his or her vision to others. Whether through staff development, shadowing, or board meeting discussions, making sure the organization's "essence" is well-rooted is undoubtedly the most important task a founder has to accomplish, and is always the first step in assuring a founder's succession and success.

A second resource about the founding experience comes from another set of nonprofit founders interviewed as part of my doctoral dissertation, *In Their Own Words: The Entrepreneurial Behavior of Nonprofit Founders.* [xxii] These lessons, both practical and poignant, are good advice to founders at every stage of the founding lifecycle.

In Their Own Words: Founders' Advice to Other Founders

1. "If you're going to found something, make sure that it's something your heart cares about, because in those dark nights, if your heart's not in it, you're not going to make it."

2. "Never lose track of the fact that you are creating something that will be owned by the community. Your job is to 'sell your shares' bit by bit so that more people can own the place. Sell all the shares until they are eventually gone, and it becomes theirs, not yours."

3. "Take your time and get the business set up properly in the beginning. Work on getting a good board as you develop the work. Partner with staff who are strong in areas where you are weak."

4. "Find a mentor who will not just tell you what to do but be there to show you how to do it."

5. "Get a board that has vision and is able to run toward the light yet still enable your own practical achievement. That's what you need in board members, and don't let them overly rely on you."

6. "Learn to read the numbers. Every good director has to learn to do that. You have to learn to look backwards financially, and then to look forward. That's how you take informed risks."

7. "When you decide to go, it helps if you have a life to move towards. If you exit with a sense of loss, you will feel incomplete."

8. "Leave at the top of your game and before people think you should. Listen to your radar systems. Give the institution enough time and enough space to articulate the future vision without you."

9. "Your board of directors is the most important link and bridge in your transition out. They need to understand the management aspects of the organization so they will have the necessary tools to hire and evaluate your successor."

10. "Before you leave, make sure the organizational history is written down and officially approved by the board."

11. "Work yourself out of a job. Look at it with the idea of training others to carry on the work. It's one thing to think 'this is mine forever.' But as a founder, it's not yours to keep."

12. "When you do leave, take a complete break. Don't hover around. Let the new person run alone."

Finally, this chapter ends with an illustrative case example, the *Avoca Literary Center* which describes the complex dynamics nonprofits experience as they make inevitable founder transitions.

CASE STUDY: The Avoca Literary Center

It was late afternoon, and Jeremy Wilcox, founder and artistic director of the Avoca Literary Center, a fifteen-year-old arts organization he'd founded to spotlight the writings of Northwestern authors, was just now arriving at his office. It had been quite a day. He'd spent the whole morning with the state Arts Board planning for the upcoming Tri-State Arts Festival that Jeremy was chairing. As an accomplished and well-published author himself, Jeremy was able to attract national press and attention for both his own Literary Center as well as the entire region. And, with his help, the region had spawned several poet-in-residence colonies over the past five years.

Jeremy was definitely an exception to the old maxim "a prophet is without honor in his own town." His ability to bring tourism and attention to this small Northwestern community had made him a local hero.

But his afternoon meeting with the board's executive committee proved he was far from a hero in their eyes. Yesterday, Jeremy had a serious confrontation with the general manager, Veronica Bellus, over his concern about the Center's financial situation. Veronica had immediately called the Center's board chair, Stuart Hartman, and threatened her resignation, making her potentially the fourth general manager in seven years to leave the Center's general manager position. Alarmed by Veronica's threatened resignation, Stuart had called an emergency executive committee meeting the following day, mandating Jeremy's presence.

Stuart, an attorney with a large regional firm, had been on the Avoca Literary Center's board for four years. As one of the board's most tenured members, he had led the search for Veronica when the previous general manager had resigned. That transition, just eighteen months ago, had been a volatile one, much debated by the board. Some board members felt the previous manager should have been given more time to improve her performance, since, after all, she was fresh out of college. Besides, they liked her, and felt that Jeremy, who had a tendency to "dump" tasks on any new administrative person rather than train them in, might have not treated her as an equal. Jeremy expected all new managers to "earn their keep" the minute they walked through the door.

Part of the problem, as Stuart reflected on it, was that, until they had hired Veronica Bellus, the Center's managers all had been junior to Jeremy in age, skill, and years in the work force. Even though they came in with the "general manager" title, they had all been inexperienced business managers rather than people with overall management experience. This kept Jeremy at the helm of the organization rather than just in the artistic driver's seat where he insisted he wanted to be, and where the board felt he needed to be if the Center was going to continue to take advantage of growth opportunities.

So, eighteen months ago, when the general manager position had opened up yet again, Stuart insisted the board take a more active role in the hiring process, and volunteered to chair the search process. Jeremy was thrilled that the board wanted to take on this responsibility. It meant one less thing for him to do.

And thus Stuart and the board developed a sub-committee charged with 1) rethinking the general manager's position and its reporting relationship; 2) developing a profile of the ideal candidate; and 3) designing new job descriptions for both the general manager and for Jeremy as the artistic director.

Most significantly, Stuart and the board had not invited Jeremy to be part of their decisions. Instead, Stuart had interviewed Jeremy, making careful note of how Jeremy perceived the general manager's function, as well as his own role as artistic director.

After several weeks, the board committee decided on two things: 1) the Center's tremendous growth opportunities required a seasoned arts administrator, and 2) the general manager should report directly to the board, rather than to Jeremy.

With the board's full consensus, the committee developed an organizational chart that clearly separated these positions, listing Jeremy as artistic director and an open general manager position. Both positions reported directly to the board.

Jeremy had swallowed hard when Stuart presented him with the new reporting format. It wasn't so much that he cared who reported to him, it was more the tone and implication of Stuart's words which, even to this day, stuck in his craw. In his matter of fact manner, Stuart had made sure Jeremy understood that the new general manager was the *board's* responsibility, not Jeremy's, and that, from now on, the position reported to the board and to the board alone. Jeremy was not to "get in the way" of the new person's operating, financial, and fundraising functions.

Within six months the board had hired Veronica Bellus, a seasoned arts administrator who'd come to the Center from a $10 million theater company in Seattle. Veronica had recently moved to Avoca with her husband, an insurance executive who'd been transferred there to open a branch office. Veronica had taken a significant pay cut to join the Center, but it was the only job in the arts in this much smaller city, and she felt lucky to have found it.

Yet, from the very start, Jeremy and Veronica had been out of sync in nearly every way. Although Veronica had reviewed the Center's audits and annual reports prior to taking the job, she was shocked to find so many projects going on given the Center's small staff. Likewise, as general manager, she had assumed her role would be more supervisory. In her former position she had *managed* the development and financial functions, not had to do them herself. This wasn't exactly what she had bargained for. Yet, she reasoned, how hard could it be? The Center was less than one tenth the size of her former budget. She could do it.

But now, here it was, six months into the new fiscal year, and except for the $1 million Jeremy had brought in from the National Humanities Commission for the Tri-State Festival, the Center itself hadn't raised any of its budgeted funds from individuals, corporations, or foundations. Veronica was painfully aware that fundraising accounted for fifty percent of the Center's annual $750,000 budget. Yet, she believed fundraising was really the board's task. That's how it had been at her last job and how all the textbooks said it should be. So she dutifully put fundraising as a topic on each month's board agenda and had even set up a fundraising committee of the board, a first for the Center.

Jeremy knew from experience that the Center needed to fundraise enough cash in the first six months of the year to cover the notoriously slow second half of the fiscal year. Given the lack of contributions, he couldn't figure out how the Center was still able to cash flow its payroll and other expenses.

Still stinging from the board's admonition to "butt out" of the operational role, he nonetheless confronted Veronica, asking how the organization was funding its operations without outside support?

As he feared, Veronica, with the finance committee's approval, had drawn down all the Center's reserves to meet expenses up through the last month. Worse yet, to cover this month's payroll, taxes, and other program expenses, she had dipped into the restricted humanities grant meant for next summer's festival. This was, she explained, a "temporary measure, until the board could get its fundraising act together."

Jeremy was livid. Although he'd never considered himself particularly skilled at finance, he knew enough to not use restricted funds for general payroll purposes, particularly funds held in fiscal agency for another organization. Bad as some of the Center's early years were, they'd never before run out of cash. Never. How ironic that the Center, with the most professional manager they'd ever had (and paying a fortune for her too, by the way), was not only out of cash, but violating funds held in trust for others.

Jeremy knew a phone call or two to old friends of the Center could probably secure emergency donations of up to $100,000. But that meant *he* would have to make the calls, and then go, hat-in-hand, to these long-term personal and organizational friends.

But why should he? The board had made it ever so clear that he was to stay out of the financial side of operations. Yet, how could he not? The Center would soon go into a major downward cash spiral, having used up its own funds, and now on the way to eroding the festival's funds as well. Although he'd faced some serious problems before, something was different now. The board was so heavily invested in Veronica and their new reporting structure that Jeremy no longer felt he had a real say in what needed to be done. In fact, he felt almost alienated from the board, even those members he had known and felt close to for years.

Although clearly different this time around, these kinds of struggles were starting to get very old. How many times had he been in this place before? Alone with his organization, in spite of his fancy general managers, who all quit in the end. Alone, despite a board of directors who was supposed to be helping him, not getting in his way. Why couldn't the Center attract competent people who took responsibility for the organization like he had for so many years?

Alone with his thoughts, the phone call had come from Stuart requesting Jeremy's presence at their emergency executive committee meeting the following afternoon.

Lifecycle Discussion Questions

1. This case represents several classic themes in organizational evolution, particularly the transition from the start-up, founder-dependent stage to a more institutional interdependence. Identify the major themes that comprise this evolution.

2. Although this case is written from Jeremy's perspective as artistic manager and founder, the board of directors also plays a central role. Was the board's impulse to create a new structural model for the general manager position correct? Do you agree with how they proceeded to develop the structure and implement it?

3. While designed with the best of intentions, the new structure apparently did not work as planned. Where did it break down? Was the breakdown structural or personal?

4. How might you have structured the organization to best take advantage of its momentum, reputation, and resources?

5. If you were Stuart or another member of the board, what would you do now in the face of this crisis? How would you ensure that your next solution would work better than the last?

6. If you were Jeremy, what would you do?

7. Should the board try to convince Veronica to stay, and if so, under what terms?

7

DEVELOPING
BOARD OWNERSHIP

Our board is like a soccer team that's never played a game. It's time we suit up, learn our positions and get ready to take the field.

*The board chair of a
growth-stage music academy*

Critical as a founder is to an organization's inception, it is the board of directors that is actually responsible for its ultimate permanence. There are many excellent texts that present the legal and functional roles, responsibilities, and duties of a nonprofit governing board. These texts, available through such sources as Board Source and most states' Attorneys General offices, are important resources for all nonprofits to understand the overall requirements of nonprofit governance at any lifecycle stage.

But from a lifecycle framework, most textbook definitions of governance reflect the functioning of *mature* boards, rather than the patterns of boards in earlier developmental cycles (*idea, start-up,* or *growth*) or those sloping downward into *decline, turnaround,* or *terminal.*

Chapter 4 listed five capacity-builders ~ programs, management, governance, resources, and systems ~ which together define capacity at each lifecycle stage. As with the other capacity components, nonprofit boards, too, mature developmentally, rather than instantly. And though most texts assume instantaneous board maturity, you and I know otherwise.

Nonprofit boards achieve maturation over a series of years, or sometimes a series of events, that together impart a collective institutional wisdom. The process is not automatic. Indeed, for some boards, maturation never occurs, while for others, the right composition and circumstances help their boards mature much sooner than the overall lifecycle stage might imply.

This chapter describes the most important and critical juncture in the board's maturation process, *the point at which the board takes collective*

Nonprofit boards achieve maturation over a series of years, or sometimes a series of events, that together impart a collective institutional wisdom. The process is not automatic. Indeed, for some, maturation never occurs, while for others, the right composition and circumstances help their boards mature much sooner than the overall lifecycle stage might imply.

ownership of the organization. Chapter 6 touched on the transference of organizational ownership from the founder's perspective. This chapter describes organizational ownership from the board's point of view. The case illustration, *Outreach, Inc.,* at the close of this chapter, exemplifies how quickly an otherwise excellent nonprofit can stumble when the board has not developed ownership congruent with the needs of its programs, management, and other capacity-building functions.

Governing the Early Lifecycle Stages

The lifecycle stage descriptions presented in Chapter 3 synopsized the role of the nonprofit board at each stage. The *start-up stage,* in particular, sets up the fundamental juxtaposition between the textbook definition of governance and the types of developmental tasks boards must work through to achieve maturity.

Board members are most likely to join a *start-up* board because of their own personal interests or connection to the organizational purpose or cause. At this stage, job one for staff and board alike is to seed the organization's purpose and programs into the community, making its presence known and appreciated. It is the rare *start-up* nonprofit board that is equally focussed on building an institution or on increasing organizational capacity.

It's when demand for the organization's services begins to take hold in the community that the first inklings of *in*-capacity begin to be noticed. Up until now, although the nonprofit may have lacked certain basic capacities, folks neither noticed nor were overly concerned. In fact, as the Christine example in Chapter 5 demonstrates, as a *start-up* manager, it never dawned on me that someone would quit a job because of lack of air-conditioned offices or state-of-the art equipment. We had an important service to deliver, with or without air-conditioning.

But now, as the growing nonprofit achieves its place on the community's radar screen, things begin to change. Board members realize that they may need to regroup. They may possibly even need to bring in different sets of skills than otherwise present, such as additional legal, marketing or personnel expertise. Some organizations may also recruit bankers or program-specific experts to strengthen their skill and community knowledge base.

Similar to the addition of new staff, some new board members will join nonprofit boards because of their love and belief in the mission. Others may have no connection to the mission but join because a friend asked them. Either way, these second-stage board members have not lived through the organizational *start-up* pains that earlier members have and consequently, come onto the board with increased expectations and a certain amount of "basics" taken for granted. For example, new board members generally expect meetings to start on time, to receive agendas in advance of the meeting, and to review minutes in a timely manner afterwords. And thus begins the board's formalization process.

Ownership, not Stewardship

But increased board professionalism will not necessarily result in board ownership. The ownership transference from executive staff to the board requires board members to "own" not only their board membership role, but, more importantly, to own the overall workings of the organization. On paper these two roles may look synonymous, but in reality the difference between the two is what *board ownership* is all about. Owning a role is a theoretical thing. Realizing that, as a board member, you are responsible for the organization's overall success and well-being, and then acting on that realization, is quite another.

> Owning the role of "board member" is a theoretical thing. Realizing that, as a board member, you are responsible for the organization's overall success and well-being, is quite another.

Figure 10: Stages of Board Ownership

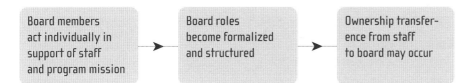

Board members act individually in support of staff and program mission → Board roles become formalized and structured → Ownership transference from staff to board may occur

A quick illustration may help. Not long ago I facilitated a board retreat of a nonprofit which, by any standards, would be considered to have a first-rate board. Responsible and committed board members consistently do their part at fundraising, monitoring the organization's strategic and financial direction, and performing all the other duties one might expect of a dream board.

One of the subjects discussed at the retreat was the imminent retirement of the agency's long-time executive director, a person beloved to those both within and outside the organization. As they stepped through the proposed transition plans, I realized that the board viewed the organization's ownership as residing in the long-term executive and were anticipating, at his departure, the ownership to transfer to the next executive.

When I raised the question of "ownership" with them, I saw the board chair's immediate flash of recognition. *I have always considered myself a good 'steward' of the organization and its mission,* she said, *but not an 'owner.' Thinking of the board's ownership role makes the proposed transition almost less frightening. It's up to us to take ultimate responsibility for carrying the organization forward, and for hiring the right executive partner.*

That was this board's first recognition of their collective organizational ownership. It was a profound moment, and one I believe they will not forget. The day after the retreat, the departing executive called to tell me that he felt this was the defining moment of the retreat, and he, too, had left the meeting with a sense of peace that the organization was now no longer in his hands, but the board's.

I want to say another word here about the all-important role of the board chair. I have come to believe that, next to the executive director, the board chair is the second most important person in building nonprofit capacity … or at least could be. Particularly in the *growth stage*, when life is coming fast and hard for the organization, and the executive has a million things on his or her plate, savvy board chairs, who *own* the board's rightful governance role and take responsibility for the board's functioning are worth their weight in gold.

As you read the following case, picture how different *Outreach, Inc.'s* situation would have been if the board (and board chair) would have developed its ownership function before the executive's transition, rather than afterwards.

CASE STUDY: Outreach, Inc.

It was 5:00 p.m. on a Tuesday evening, and the board of Outreach, Inc. had just gathered in executive session to discuss yet the latest in a series of crises which the organization faced since replacing its long-term executive director, Jack O'Connor, six months earlier.

The latest crisis was financial. Although just nine months-ago there had been an operating reserve fund of more than $100,000, the organization could not meet its Friday payroll. Board members knew that immediate steps must be taken to address the current cash shortage, yet some speculated they may have a more fundamental problem on their hands: the new executive, in whom they had placed such confidence, may not be up to the job. But where had they gone wrong?

The search committee was comprised of the board's most savvy business people who gave up hours of time to participate in the search process. Considerable discussion had been given to the needs of the agency and, in particular, current management weaknesses board members hoped to correct through the hiring process. Although sad to be losing their long-time director and friend, deep inside, many were excited about the opportunity this opening gave them.

Over the last fifteen years, Outreach, Inc., had grown from an out-patient counseling service to a multi-service agency for emotionally disturbed adolescents. Jack was one of its founders and had a reputation for bedrock honesty, integrity and solid programming. His first commitment was always to clients and their families, and, because he came out of a clinical background, he saw himself more as a "counselor" than a "manager." Nonetheless, under his leadership the organization had grown from a donation-only income stream to a $3 million program, sustained primarily by contracts with multiple counties and insurance companies. Clients from around the country were clamoring to get into the program, the organization had built its reserves, and its reputation was solid.

But despite these successes, many of the board had grown somewhat disenchanted with Jack, who didn't do things in the traditional way. Board members who sat on other nonprofit boards thought Outreach should do more fundraising with local foundations. Others wanted the organization to do more marketing and public relations events like black-tie benefits and annual appeals. And though this had been a running issue through the years, it had come to a head about a year earlier, when a national network entertainment show had contacted Jack to do a feature on teenage prostitution, hoping to spotlight kids from Outreach, Inc.'s treatment program. Jack had immediately said "no." Hearing about this later, the board had reprimanded Jack for being so shortsighted. A chance to bring national attention to their small local program was something that could have been finessed into a golden opportunity.

But that was all water under the bridge since Jack had resigned several months later, and from a slate of three outstanding candidates, the board chose Bill Lewis, the applicant with the most marketing and public relations experience.

Bill came to Outreach, Inc. having been the administrator of a small hospital in the Southeast. Although he had no experience in the field of adolescent psychology, he was a licensed hospital administrator with a polished style and commanding presence. Bill had been the board's unanimous choice. His grand plans and ambitious approach were just the opposite of Jack's more low-key and down-to-earth style. Bill seemed to have the right stuff to take Outreach, Inc. to new heights, especially with funders, donors, and the general public.

But now, as the board looked back over the last six months, they weren't so sure. Everything seemed to be falling apart. The clinical director, a woman deeply respected by clients, staff and referral sources, had quit, citing irreconcilable differences with the new director. Reserves had been drawn down to renovate and refurnish the administrative offices, a decision that seemed appropriate at the time, but now appeared shortsighted. Worse yet, referrals had fallen off drastically, despite a four-color brochure and video the agency had just completed. For the first time in five years, Outreach, Inc. had empty beds.

Now in executive session, the board wondered where they had gone wrong, and what should be done about it.

Several of the board members felt that this was a transitional problem, not at all unusual given the long history of the former director and the big shoes left to fill. They argued that although the new director had made what now appeared to be some errors in financial judgment, with coaching, training and support, he would be all right in the end. The president of the board, a corporate management trainer, volunteered to set up weekly meetings with the new director to coach and provide a sounding board for the director's decisions.

Other board members were not so generous. They reasoned that although the organization had weathered many storms in its early and mid-years, Outreach, Inc. had never experienced client recruitment or dissatisfaction problems. Now, even though the new marketing efforts would bring about the potential for national referrals, Outreach could not attract clients from its own state. Moreover, its reputation seemed to be suffering with the departure of both the executive director and the clinical director. No matter what you called it, they reasoned, if an agency loses clients from its own community, isn't that a sign of trouble?

The board was at a stalemate. They'd moved the director over a thousand miles to take this job. He had only been here for six months and yet, in that time, clients, money, and reputation seemed to be slipping away fast. Some felt the organization should cut its losses, let the director go, and start the search again. Others felt the problem was transitional and that the board president's offer to coach and become more involved in the day-to-day decisions would help the new director learn the job while providing the board with some security that the agency was, in fact, in good hands.

Realizing this was too big a decision to make at this one meeting, the board strategized on how it would solve the payroll problem and agreed to meet in special session again two weeks later.

Lifecycle Discussion Questions

1. In what life cycle stage is Outreach, Inc.? Was there a shifting of stages during the six months described?

2. Did the board "go wrong" in the search process?

3. Are the organization's current calamities transitional growing pains or more serious problems which need correction?

4. If you were on this board, which way would you vote?

5. If you were charged with developing the next five immediate action steps to resolve this organization's problems, what would they be?

This NONPROFIT LIFECYCLES © 2001 case study is purely fictional. Any resemblance or similarity to an existing non-profit corporation, or persons of the same name, is coincidental and unintended.

8
BUILDING YOUR BENCH

We don't know who we are until we see what we can do.

Martha Grimes

A few years ago, the John D. and Catherine T. MacArthur Foundation in Chicago convened a group of "high-performance" grantees to participate in a roundtable discussion to articulate their best practices. To the foundation's surprise, these nonprofit executives universally cited the importance of "bench strength" ~ having solid people in second, third, and even fourth-level positions ~ as one of the chief contributors to their organizational success.

Developing "bench strength" (a sports metaphor meaning having multiple people "on the bench" capable of successfully performing in the game), is a timely topic for both individual nonprofits and the sector as a whole. With 80,000 or so new nonprofits coming into being each year *(Board Source)*, and the mass exit of the boomer-generation from the work place over the next decade, some estimate that, between 2007 and 2016, the nonprofit sector will need to attract as many as 640,000 new senior managers *(Bridgespan Group*[xxiii]*)*.

With these dynamics in mind, I want to link the concept of *bench-strength* with an equally timely topic, *succession planning.*

Bench Building ~ Succession Planning from the Bottom Up

It is almost impossible to pick up a nonprofit journal without seeing some mention of succession planning. And, more frequently than not, the article's focus is on preparing for the CEO's departure.

Yet, the concept of succession planning is far more widely applicable than the executive transition alone. Indeed, when approached from the bottom-up rather than top-down, succession planning is the equivalent of bench building.

My former employer, LarsonAllen, had a great term for bench building. We called it *building a succession organization.* The concept started as a leadership development strategy that soon became a fundamental part of the firm's organizational culture as well as a framework for investing in our greatest asset, our *human capital.*

Applying this valuable concept to the nonprofit sector, a succession organization is one that:

- Identifies, recruits, trains and retains "star" employees

- Values and encourages a culture of achievement at each level of employment

- Promotes upward opportunity

- Anticipates turnover in all positions so that employee departure *on any level* will not negatively affect the organization's performance

Succession organizations have other things in common as well. Most fundamentally, they understand their lifecycle stage. They hire people whose skill and experience are in keeping with the job requirements *and* whose work personality and expectations are consistent with the organization's lifecycle stage. In lifecycle language, we call that "hiring for fit." Anyone who has ever hired someone who looked good on paper but ended up not "fitting into" the organization can certainly relate. (See the "Christine" example cited in Chapter 5)

Succession organizations also recruit top-notch people at every level of the organization and take steps to develop them into future leaders. Ironically, the same organizations that put considerable effort into hiring senior-level managers often pay far less attention to entry-level recruiting. The more you can attract talented people at all organizational levels, the stronger your bench will be.

Succession organizations retain their star employees and make meaningful investments in them. Rather than one-sized training or incentive programs, they seek input from staff on all levels about what incentives they might most appreciate. Often the most meaningful reward systems are also the least costly.

Building cross-disciplinary and cross-trained teams is another way to build a succession organization and contribute to bench building. Likewise creating "stepping-up" opportunities for staff on all levels provides an addi-

When approached from the bottom-up rather than top-down, succession planning is the equivalent of bench building.

tional way for staff to showcase their strength and commitment, as well as provide management with a new way to evaluate talent and ambition.

However, even the most attentive bench-building practices won't make the wrong person right for a job. This becomes doubly hard when that same person is a loyal employee who has invested heavily in the organization and continues to want to do so. He or she has done nothing wrong, but the organization's needs have changed in ways that no longer match their skills. This is, of course, one of the most difficult dilemmas organizations face at any lifecycle stage. These types of fit issues, though, are particularly pronounced in the *start-up* and *growth stages* where, so often, the organization's needs are changing rapidly, and the type of person once right for the *start-up* is less likely to have the skills, experience or fit required to keep pace with the changing organization.

The remainder of this chapter discusses the predictable personnel challenges *start-up* and *growth* stage nonprofits are likely to face as they develop their bench, formalize roles, and match employee skill and fit to job requirements. I single out these two stages since they represent the periods when nonprofits generally move from a personal attachment to employees to a more professional and defined formalization of roles.

This chapter ends with a real-life (albeit fictional) case study of a *growth-stage* organization that "outgrew" the skills of a devoted employee and how they dealt with it.

Building Your Bench in the Start-up and Growth Stages

The open-to-opportunity nature of the *start-up stage* generally attracts wonderful, big-hearted generalists eager and willing to give their all in support of the cause. Later, as the organization changes and begins to specialize, these "can-do" generalists, although once so essential, may not have the types of specific competencies required to move the organization forward.

As new staff are hired, particularly if they have been hired for a specific and defined job, they generally come into the organization with a much higher set of expectations than those who had previously helped to build the organization so far. New employees expect job descriptions, an organizational chart, personnel policies, and a certain degree of amenities that *start-ups* are accustomed to living without. They also expect to be paid on time, to have paid vacations, and maybe even to have an organizational career path.

These changing characteristics of first-stage to second-stage staff is reflective of the transition from the *start-up* to *growth stage*. This transition represents one of the most important points of demarcation between these two stages: the first formal development of job descriptions, role definitions, and reporting responsibilities for staff.

By definition, the *growth stage* occurs when demand for a nonprofit's service outstrips its capacity to perform. This increase in service almost always requires additional staff and can often mean hiring several at a time. With the addition of new staff comes the need to reallocate job roles and responsibilities. *Start-up* staff who have become accustomed to their multiple roles are often not at all inclined to "give up" parts of their job to a newcomer. (Although founders often get a bad rap for wanting to keep everything within their control, it's often just as hard for first-staff to make the same kinds of hand-offs.)

Formalizing Roles

On paper, the formalization of job roles and responsibilities is but one more milestone on the strategic path to *maturity*. But for first-stage staff, whose loyalty, willingness, and flexibility have, up until now, been one of the organization's greatest assets, formalization can be replete with hard feelings. Up until now, most staff reported directly to the single executive. The organization may have even operated like a family. If there was an organizational chart of any kind, its boxes were filled with individual *names* rather than *positions*.

In second-stage management, the organization becomes more dependent on positions, and less dependent on individual people. Rather than hiring a person to take *"Mary's"* place, in second-stage management, Mary's functions are bundled into a job description, and a person is hired to fill that *position*. The further along in the lifecycle stage, the more likely it is that the new person hired will have held a similar position before, thus bringing added depth to the agency.

In addition to the growing pains brought on by formalization, the transition from *start-up* to *growth* brings other staff challenges as well. For the first time, the whole organization, from the founder to the newest staff, realizes there is now something to lose. Staff become less forgiving of the founder, if still there, and much more likely to start asking "why." Communication, too, becomes more formal, causing first-staff, once energetic partners in the development phase, to now feel displaced by more "professional" staff who, they feel, neither know the programs as well as they, nor all it took to get there.

These staff dynamics represent very difficult, but normal, dynamics that accompany the *growth stage*. There is a fine balance, particularly in a nonprofit, between respecting the hard work and loyalty of first staff, yet

For first-stage staff, whose loyalty, willingness and flexibility have, up until now, been the organization's greatest asset, formalization can be replete with hard feelings.

still embracing the professional capabilities of second-stage staff. It takes a tremendous amount of foresight, skill, and tact to effectively manage the transition between first- and second-stage management.

Equally important to this transition is the need for founders and other managers to train new staff, and then, once trained, to let go and delegate. Indeed, it is the desire and need to delegate because there is too much to do that generally causes a manager to realize they don't have the right skill on their "bench" of first-stage staff to effectively delegate the evolving program or administrative work that needs to be done.

With the transition to second-stage staff frequently comes the creation of a *middle management*, a new level of responsibility that disperses organizational ownership from one to many. With the addition of a middle range of managers, nonprofits begin to establish the beginnings of institutional depth and organizational capacity, which sets up a third-stage transition and yields the kind of bench strength found prevalent in MacArthur's best practice grantees.

The following case describes many of the dynamics found in the transition between first- and second-stage staff management. Just as in life, the personal dynamics of the situation intermix with the organizational requirements, providing a complex and thought provoking illustration of lifecycle dynamics in action.

CASE STUDY: The Brighton City Community Foundation

It was four o'clock in the morning, and, for the past two hours, Elizabeth Wakefield had been lying awake ruminating over the events of the day. As executive director of the Brighton City Community Foundation, Elizabeth had begun to refer to these sleepless nights as the day's "golden moments." Far from dreading these bouts of insomnia, she had come to rely on them as uninterrupted time to think about and strategize her next day's activities.

Elizabeth had been the Foundation's executive director for the past three years, a period of time in which the Foundation's assets had grown from $2 million to $8 million. Its subsequent ability to become a community presence had increased substantially, as well.

Founded almost fifty years ago, the Foundation had remained somewhat dormant until just five years earlier when a small board of local business leaders had taken it upon themselves to resurrect the community foundation, and hired Robyn Richards as executive secretary to the board. Robyn was a real go-getter, and under the board's specific direction, was able to assist in the implementation and execution of their positioning efforts.

When the decision was made to hire an executive director for the Foundation, many of the board members even considered Robyn. But, in the end, they had agreed that Robyn, although an administrative whiz, did not possess the entrepreneurial or leadership skills the Foundation required. Instead they had hired Elizabeth Wakefield who, sensitive to the loyalty and efficiency with which Robyn had served the Foundation, made a concerted effort to work with Robyn in a "team" rather than "boss" fashion.

And what a team they were! Within three years, through their combined efforts, the Brighton City Community Foundation had attracted a board of committed business and other community leaders, raised an additional $6 million dollars in permanent assets, and sponsored numerous community events through its "Philanthropic Services" initiative. And based on the news they had received yesterday, this was just the beginning.

The Brighton City Community Foundation had just been awarded a challenge grant of $1 million from a large national foundation interested in jump-starting emerging community foundations. With the challenge grant came another $200,000 in operating support payable over four years which would allow the Foundation to hire another staff person for whatever purposes necessary.

To attract this funding, Elizabeth had sketched out a potential organizational chart (the first one the Foundation had ever had) which showed herself as the Foundation's president, supported by a newly created program manager position, and an administrative manager position, drawn on an equal level with the program manager. In fact, Elizabeth did not see the administrative role equal to the program manager's, but deference to Robyn's important history with the Foundation seemed to dictate placing these positions on an equal footing.

But now that the money had been awarded, it was clear that Robyn had no interest in the administrative job at all. She rightly assumed that the Foundation's future energy would be focused around new programming, and that's where she wanted to be! Citing her tenure, loyalty and friendship with Elizabeth and members of the board, she declared herself a candidate for the program position.

This left Elizabeth, who valued Robyn's expertise and friendship, in a real quandary. Without Robyn, the board and Elizabeth would never have been able to make such quick progress toward the Foundation's goals. Nor, for that matter, would they have been able to meet the deadline or materials requirements of their national funder. Robyn was the organized person in the office. She had created a system for everything. As the first point of contact, board and community members loved her pleasant, efficient manner. There was no doubt about it, she had always been a complete joy to work with and a real treasure for the Foundation, at least until now. Robyn was making it abundantly clear that unless she was chosen for the program manager position, she would feel passed over, and be forced to quit.

Elizabeth was caught between a rock and a hard place. Robyn was her friend and confidante. Over the years they had shared everything about the Foundation, including an occasional giggle about the quirks of some of their board members. But Elizabeth knew that Robyn would not bring the abilities or experience to the new program position that the Foundation needed to capitalize on its current good fortune. Elizabeth and the board wanted to grow the assets of the Foundation to $25 million over the next ten years, and to do that they needed a savvy program manager who was creative and experienced.

But neither did Elizabeth want to lose Robyn, and that was what had awakened her tonight. So, rather than lying in bed stewing, Elizabeth got up, went to her home computer and created two job descriptions, one for the program manager and the other for an administrative manager. Elizabeth took care to "upgrade" the administrative manager responsibilities, and even included several duties she herself was now performing.

Later that morning, although she had been given complete authority to conduct the hiring process, Elizabeth phoned the board president for an appointment. In her meeting with him, she showed him the job descriptions and explained that quite possibly she might end up hiring for two positions rather than one. The board chair expressed reservations about setting up a situation that would lead to Robyn's departure, but advised Elizabeth to do what she thought best for the Foundation.

Elizabeth went back to the office and gave Robyn both job descriptions, asking her to take some time over the rest of the week to reconsider staying on as the Foundation's administrative manager.

At the end of the day, in a fit of emotion, Robyn told Elizabeth again that she would only consider the program position. Elizabeth advised Robyn that the following Sunday she was placing an employment ad for the two positions in the local paper. Robyn would be free to apply for either position, and would be considered along with all applicants, but Elizabeth, looking out for the long-term interests of the Foundation, intended to hire the best applicant for each job.

For the first night in a week, convinced that she had handled this situation in the best possible manner, Elizabeth slept the night uninterrupted. However, when she came to work the following day, she found Robyn's letter of resignation on her desk.

Lifecycle Discussion Questions

1. Why had Robyn resigned?

2. In what lifecycle stage was the Brighton City Community Foundation?

3. What do you think of how Elizabeth handled this situation?

4. Should the board chair have taken a more active role?

5. Given the lifecycle stage, should Elizabeth have handled this situation differently?

6. Should Elizabeth have reneged and let Robyn become the program manager?

This NONPROFIT LIFECYCLES © 2001 case study is purely fictional. Any resemblance or similarity to an existing nonprofit corporation, or persons of the same name, is coincidental and unintended.

9

EFFECTING A TURNAROUND

There's a big difference between knowing what has to be done to turn an organization around and being able to effectively lead the board and staff through the necessary changes. We've known for years what's wrong. We just can't seem to find our way out of it.

The long-time board member of a declining organization

Have you ever wondered why some organizations, in the face of crisis or set-back, quickly make the necessary course corrections to move forward, while others steadfastly stay their original course? One of the toughest challenges of being a nonprofit manager is discerning the big problems from the little ones which have the potential to become big. Too frequently, nonprofits get so locked into their internal challenges that they can't see the proverbial forest for the trees.

This chapter is about organizational decline and how to get out of it. It's not a pretty subject. In fact, you might find that it's a bit negative for your tastes. But *turnaround* is an important lifecycle stage, and it doesn't happen without first embracing those troubling, negative factors of *decline*.

Although nonprofits can enter the *decline stage* from almost any life-cycle stage, the progression generally goes from *maturity* to *decline*, or from *start-up* to *decline*. When *start-ups* decline it is almost always because of capacity issues, frequently related to management (sometimes a founder) that is not willing to let the organization mature beyond personal inclinations or abilities. Thus an almost crippling paralysis ensues in which nothing either changes or progresses.

But for nonprofits that enter *decline* having once been mature, the situation is different. The *decline stage* occurs when nonprofits forget the tenuous balance between mission and market. Rather than keeping their eyes focussed on community needs and demands, the declining organization focuses instead on continuing its own programs and interests, usually at all costs. As the world turns around them, *decline-stage* groups, comfortable with the way things are, continue to conduct business in the usual manner oblivious or deliberately ignoring what's happening in their field or marketplace.

The Mindset of Decline

Decline-stage nonprofits have an inward focus that is concerned more with the needs of staff and management than those of clients. A certain rigidity has set in, with the emphasis on "what we do and how we do it" rather than who needs it and why it's needed.

For *decliners,* it's all about them. Staff and management become locked into their own tried and true methods and seldom seek evaluative client feedback. This can result in a form of self-indulgence that later, as the stage progresses, deteriorates into an organizational paralysis having gone so long without self-renewing activities.

Declining organizations justify their thought processes and decisions by their reputation and community position. Rather than bringing new insight or approaches to the table, they continue to recycle traditional programs whether needed or not.

Organizations in *decline* don't like to change, and they frequently fail to learn from their mistakes. Denial and blame usually accompany *decline.* Denial can take many forms, from making excuses for losing program contracts or clients, to blaming decreased funding or revenues on an outside phenomenon. Either way, rather than acknowledge and adapt to the circumstance, the organization ignores or makes excuses for it.

Most declining organizations are stuck and don't know any other way of moving except in the same ruts created in the past. Consequently, it usually takes an outside intervention to help dislodge them from the status quo. This intervention typically comes in the form of a financial crisis. There's something about money that seems to get people's attention in a way few other problems can.

Although crisis will usually kick even the most depressed organization into gear, crisis alone can't effect a *turnaround,* or even renewal. In fact, through years of practice, many declining organizations have learned to crisis-manage, and indeed, even manipulate crisis to their advantage. Their failure to take anticipatory, course-corrective action on the front end of a problem results in an eventual crisis that forces their re-action on the back-end. In this way, crisis becomes the declining organization's ally, since it allows them to rally the troops, time and again, and create the type of adrenaline rush which proves they are still alive.

The *decline stage* occurs when nonprofits forget the tenuous balance between mission and market. Rather than keeping their eyes focussed on community needs and demands, the declining organization focuses instead on continuing its own programs and interests, usually at all costs. As the world turns around them, *decline-stage* groups, comfortable with the way things are, continue to conduct business in the usual manner, oblivious or deliberately ignoring what's happening in their field or marketplace.

Five Preconditions for Successful Turnaround

So, how do organizations get out of decline? Experience suggests five interlocking conditions that together form the ingredients for successful nonprofit turnaround:

- *A committed champion.* Turnaround doesn't happen without an inside champion, someone committed to what the organization could be and discouraged about what it has become. The champion becomes the change agent and takes personal responsibility for the successful repositioning of the organization. Although reliant upon facts, the internal champion trusts his or her instinct about what is wrong, and takes decisive action for what to do about it.

  Internal champions are believable. They possess the kind of "spark" capable of re-kindling board members, staff, and funders' interest and commitment to the organization. At the same time, they act quickly and decisively to get a grip on the organization's problems and put at least a temporary fix in place to stem the downward spiral.

  The artful internal champion will orchestrate internal change without the slash and burn tactics sometimes associated with corporate turnarounds. In nonprofits, there's no place for "guerilla" tactics, "chainsaw massacres," and other macho antics the term *turnaround* has come to signify. Rather, the successful nonprofit turnaround is frequently led by someone whose credibility, skill, and respect for the mission and its people are so genuine that they elevate the turnaround to an art form.

- *A symbolic breaking point.* Successful turnarounds are generally triggered by organizational action, either internally or externally induced, that becomes the symbolic breaking point, a reminder of *what we can never let happen again.*

  The breaking point itself may not be the biggest crisis the organization has ever faced, but it represents the most important moment in the eventual turnaround. Long after the turnaround is accomplished, it is the breaking point that people remember, that symbolic moment when someone decided *things are going to be different.*

- *Internalization.* Internalization is a psychological term for understanding a situation well enough that you can take its lessons to heart. I think of it as the "getting it" factor. Internalization is critical to the effective turnaround. It describes an organization's

FIVE INGREDIENTS FOR A SUCCESSFUL NONPROFIT TURNAROUND:

- A committed champion
- A symbolic breaking point
- Internalization
- Strategic and administrative competence
- Commitment to behavior change

willingness to face both the cause and effect of its problems, not with lip service, but in a way that demonstrates a profound understanding and attitude shift (see Chapter 11 for a further discussion of this topic).

Before the effective turnaround can take hold, somebody internal to the organization has to "get it." They may not know how to get out of their troubles, but they're willing to own what got them there and commit to going forward in a different way.

- *Strategic and administrative competence.* Whereas internalization is about will, competence is about skill. Successful turnarounds require both. There are many instances when an organization actually understands the cause of its decline, but doesn't have the competence to pull out of the situation.

Effective turnarounds require both strategic and administrative competence, since these are the two areas that are generally most off-base. *Strategic turnaround* involves a change in organizational direction, rather than a restructuring of the financial position. A *financial turnaround* is a more short-term strategy that focuses on the economic levers and financial practices that control an organization's financial fate, like increasing revenues and decreasing costs, getting a grip on payables and receivables, and otherwise stemming the bleeding. A financial turnaround assumes that the nonprofit's mission, program, market, or business strategies still work, but that something has gone awry in the management process.

- *Commitment to behavior change.* Effective turnarounds also require a commitment to behavior changes on the part of management, board, and staff members. This is the action component. And because behavior change frequently hurts (a lot), this is often the most difficult of the five preconditions to operationalize.

But as the saying goes, if it doesn't hurt it isn't changing. So, nonprofits truly committed to turnaround will need to operate differently so they send a walk-the-talk signal that it isn't business as usual. To become habitual, it is especially important for behavioral change to be led from the top and by example. Staff and outside investors quickly realize whether turnaround strategies are merely lip service or true change.

Becoming the Catalyst for Change

Although each of the five components ~ a committed champion, symbolic breaking point, internalization, strategic and administrative competence, and habitual behavior change ~ must be present for the turnaround to "take," the foundational base of these five components is the committed champion who becomes the catalyst for change.

Sometimes the catalyst is a board member, often a new member who joins what he or she thinks is a healthy board, yet quickly realizes things aren't what they seemed. It may also be a new executive, program, or administrative director who blows the whistle on organizational underachievement. In some cases it may even be a grantmaker, who, after years of looking the other way, decides to call time-out on the status quo.

One thing is certain. Although managers at the helm of a *declining* organization can frequently lead their organizations through *regeneration,* they can seldom, if ever, orchestrate its *turnaround. Turnaround is nearly always catalyzed by someone other than the current positional leader.*

Board members have the best shot at triggering institutional change and creating the most long-lasting potential for making it stick. In some circumstances, *turnaround* occurs from the inside out. This usually happens with the hiring of a new executive. Foundations, too, can play a role in an organizational turnaround, sometimes in their role as concerned grantmaker, and also through investing in the ultimate turnaround plan. Chapter 11 further explores the concept of organizational change from a grantmaker's perspective.

Both nonprofits and foundations will recognize the dynamics of lifecycle *decline* in the following case, the *Tri-County Employment Alliance,* which also presents an opportunity to discuss the actions necessary to effect a successful *turnaround.*

CASE STUDY: The Tri-County Employment Alliance

Janet Turner was in turmoil. She had just returned to the office after attending her third board meeting of the Tri-County Employment Alliance, a prestigious nonprofit organization whose mission was to help low-income women achieve full economic and employment potential.

Janet had joined the board with great eagerness and affinity for the Alliance's mission. She had married young, divorced, and struggled economically to get to where she was now, ten years later, a successful accountant in a major CPA firm. Since she herself had relied on government programs to subsidize her schooling and childcare bills, Janet felt a volunteer position on the Alliance's board was a good way to "give back" to the community the benefits she had received. There was an added networking advantage, too, since all the Alliance's sixteen board members were high-powered community leaders, CEO's of major corporations, bankers, attorneys, and financial types, like herself.

But now, back in her office after the board meeting, something didn't seem right. Today the board had been asked to approve a budget twenty-five percent larger than last year's. It wasn't so much the budget growth that bothered Janet. Rather, she found herself concerned that, now, ten months into this fiscal year, the Alliance was nearly $75,000 short of its budget goals for the year. Being new to the board, she had to summon up all her courage to ask if other board members were concerned about being off budget by $75,000.

The board treasurer, the senior controller at a major corporation, had a quick explanation. Early in the budget year, right before Janet had joined the board, the local county had, without warning, cut back on its services to adults in favor of job programs for teenagers. "We've all learned that this is how it works with nonprofits, particularly those funded by government grants. You'll get used to it," he said. "It's all part of the nonprofit experience."

The executive director, who'd been with the agency twelve years, explained that they intended to make up this year's revenue difference in fundraising, and wait to see its effect on next year's budget.

Janet didn't know much about either nonprofit politics or fundraising, but she still couldn't understand why, if the board knew about this situation nearly a year ago, they hadn't modified the current year's budget.

Although dwindling county support was troubling, the board was most enthusiastic about the fundraising prospects the director had outlined, particularly the "phone-athon" which the agency had scheduled immediately after the first of the year. This was the first time they had ever done such a thing, but several board members sat on other boards and reported great success there. Based on others' experience, the Alliance felt it could raise up to $100,000, which would defray the current year's county contract loss, and maybe even provide funds for next year.

Furthermore, the board had decided to make a party out of it. One of the members, a stockbroker, had obtained use of her corporate offices and phones. Her corporation had agreed to cater a pre-phoning party with a Southwestern theme. It was clear to Janet that this was a board that enjoyed and respected each other, and saw the phone-athon as another opportunity to get together for a good cause.

Janet decided to make an appointment with the board chair to put her concerns in perspective. She was sure she understood the financial situation correctly but felt, since she was new, and none of the other board members seemed to be concerned, she must be missing something. Furthermore, Janet already felt slightly chastised by the treasurer for questioning fiscal matters at the last meeting. She didn't want to appear foolish again.

The board chair, who had been on the board for six years and was a respected community volunteer, welcomed Janet's visit but confessed that she really did not understand the financial side of the operations. She relied on the board's corporate finance people to raise a red flag when there were problems. The chair assured Janet of her utmost confidence in the current executive director. The previous executive director, the Alliance's founder, was a brilliant and charismatic woman who had put the agency on the map, but was also "scattered" and had not paid enough attention to staff morale, or established any organizational policies or procedures. It was the new executive director who had brought order to the agency. She had also recruited all the high-powered board members, and she knew how to keep them motivated by giving them just enough information to feel useful, but not overwhelmed with operational details.

The board chair admonished Janet not to take things too seriously, and reminded her that the board's role was not to micro-manage. "Everything will work out," she said. "It always does."

At the following month's board meeting, the increased budget was approved with high hopes that the phone-athon would be the winner it promised to be. Two months later, the night of the "phoning party," several board members were absent due to other conflicts, and since most of the members present weren't used to asking for money over the phone, only one-quarter of the list got called. The evening ended on a terrible note. Not only had the event fallen far short of its desired results, but board members were shocked at how distasteful the phone-calling procedure had turned out to be. Even though they still had three-quarters of the names left to call, none of them wanted anything more to do with this type of fundraising, and said so at the next month's board meeting.

Half of the board meeting was taken up with sharing stories from the phone-athon. Finally, Janet could stand it no longer. She posed the question, "What will be the impact of our failure to raise $100,000, not just on our current fiscal-year's budget, but also on the one we just approved?"

When the board chair referred the problem to the finance committee for review, Janet spoke:

> "I know I am new, but as a board member committed to women's employment
> issues, I am concerned about what seems to be a downhill financial spiral
> the Alliance has been in during the nine months I have been on the board. I
> realize you all have more history than I with the agency, but it appears that
> our client numbers have declined considerably, yet we still employ the same
> number of staff. I recommend that we engage in a financial and strategic
> restructuring process which takes a hard look at our market and our own
> internal capabilities to serve those in need of our services."

Although Janet's suggestion was met with polite approval, it was clear that she had rankled several of the board members, and especially the executive director. Knowing that the only way to ensure objectivity was to have the organizational assessment conducted by an outside firm, Janet suggested that board members seek contributions from their respective corporations to hire an outside consulting firm that would report to a small committee which she herself would chair, if the board so wished.

Armed with the appropriate approvals, Janet and her committee met with the executive director to get input on the internal and external issues to be analyzed. She also laid out her expectation that management and staff cooperate fully with the consultants.

Weeks went by, the organizational assessment occurred, and produced the following report:

- At least twelve other organizations in the city provided services similar to the Alliance. Most were new and had emerged as a reaction to the Alliance's programs, which were considered out-of-date and particularly irrelevant to minority and low-income communities.

- Alliance staff and programs, though well-intentioned, were not results-oriented. Classes were offered on how to get a job, but there was no job bank or placement service available to clients, causing them to forego the Alliance's programs in favor of other more full-service shops.

- For the last several years, the county had tried to encourage the Alliance to broaden its programming to serve young adults as well as women, but to no avail. The Alliance staff vigorously defended their need to continue programming to women in the same style that had made them effective in the first place.

- Although payroll and payroll taxes had been paid on time, other payables were mounting up. In some cases, outstanding bills were over six months old. The agency simply did not have enough money to meet its expenses. Key staff, including the executive director, did not have a grip on financial operations. Not only this, but the auditor's recommendations to conduct a cost analysis of programs and make cuts accordingly had also been ignored.

- The executive director's mother had just moved to an assisted living facility, and staff meetings inevitably turned into support groups concerned more with personal than organizational problems. Although staff members felt respected and valued by the agency, there was little personal accountability for department goals or results with clients or programs.

The board found the findings of this report painful, but compelling. Having pondered the report's implications in executive session, they later shared it with the executive director who requested time to prepare a rebuttal.

Lifecycle Discussion Questions

1. In what lifecycle stage is the Tri-County Alliance? What organizational characteristics support your stage-placement?

2. How would you describe Janet's role with the Alliance? Although new to the board, why did she speak up?

3. Describe the board's relationship with the Alliance. Why had the financially savvy board members not asked the same questions as Janet?

4. Would you characterize the Alliance's board as competent?

5. Having received the consultant's report, what action plan would you suggest the Alliance take?

This NONPROFIT LIFECYCLES © 2001 case study is purely fictional. Any resemblance or similarity to an existing non-profit corporation, or persons of the same name, is coincidental and unintended.

Part Three: CAPACITY GRANTMAKING

10

VALUE-ADDED INVESTING

An ounce of performance is worth pounds of promises.

Mae West

The first two sections of this book established the conceptual and practical definition of nonprofit capacity within a lifecycle framework. Written for nonprofits, foundations, and academics, these preceding chapters outlined the "normal" characteristics, patterns, and challenges that accompany each of the seven lifecycle stages, and presented several case examples to illustrate how the lifecycle approach works in practice.

This final section of *NONPROFIT LIFECYCLES* discusses how foundations and other donors can use the lifecycles approach to make value-added investments in nonprofit capacity ~ a subject that has come to be known in philanthropic circles as "capacity building."

The hand-in-glove relationship of capacity and mission sustainability has become far more widely understood in the seven years since publishing the earlier edition of *NONPROFIT LIFECYCLES*. More foundations are realizing that goals of *high performance*, *best practice*, and *organizational effectiveness* are wholly dependent on a nonprofit's capacity, and without that capacity, nonprofits can't make an enduring mark on society's well-being.

Earlier in this text, I defined "capacity" as *an organization's ability to achieve balance or alignment between its programs and the management, governance, financial, and other structural requirements necessary to support these programs at each stage of life.* I also offered the "table leg" metaphor as a quick visual for how capacity provides a solid base for both mission and program. Thinking of capacity as "legs" serves another purpose as well. It keeps capacity *real.* Just by looking at the table, it's obvious that programs

Although terms like *best practice*, *high performance*, and *effectiveness* are each important in their own right, they are not synonymous with organizational capacity. Rather, they are dependent on it. Capacity is the anchor for nonprofit performance. Without it, nonprofits can't hope to achieve high performance or make an enduring mark on society's well-being.

and mission can only be as strong as the capacity legs that support them.

Figure 3: Nonprofit Capacity ~ "Table Legs" Supporting Mission and Programs

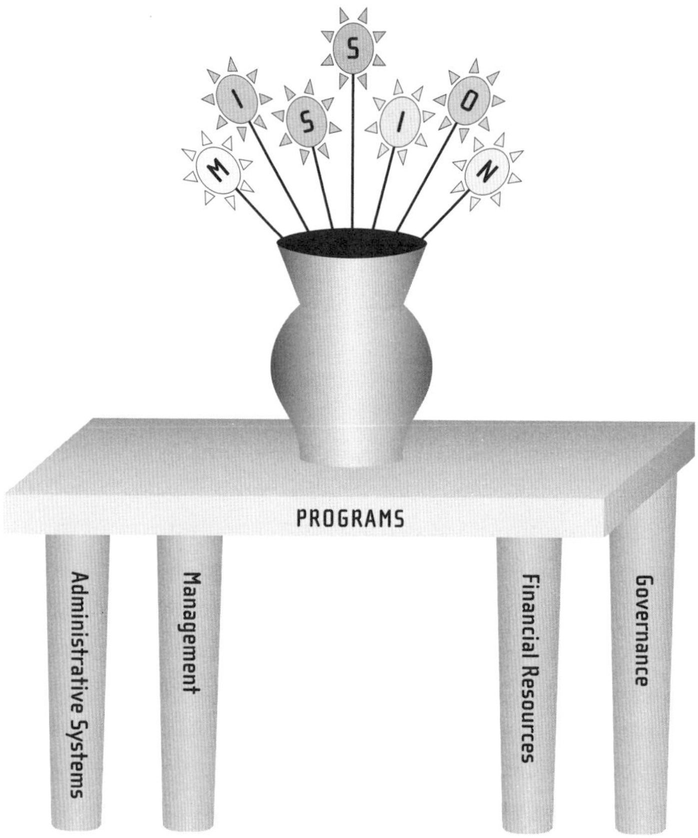

If *capacity* is about organizational competence, then *capacity-building* is about strengthening the organizational platform upon which programs and missions rest.

This book is all about establishing the importance of capacity as a ground-floor concept that requires hands-on engagement. When placed in the theoretical context of *capacity building,* we can sometimes forget its rolled-up-shirt-sleeves dimension. The epigraph at the beginning of this book says it all. *In theory, there is no difference between theory and practice. But in practice there is.*

In theory, capacity-building philanthropy is a terrific idea, and an idea whose time has come. But the types of management, governance, financial, and systems improvements nonprofits must attain to achieve operational and strategic competence are generally anything but theoretical. Nonprofit capacity requires practical solutions, grounded in solid diagnosis, to produce organizations that are strong, durable, and capable.

Given the scarcity of internal resources nonprofits generally have to self-invest in strategic direction or operational improvements, capacity-building grants become an important resource for strengthening and, in some cases, intervening in nonprofit capacity.

This chapter outlines several ways foundations and other investors have used lifecycle diagnostics to engage in capacity-building grantmaking. Out of dozens of possible examples, I've provided a handful of illustrations meant to illuminate the lifecycle concept, rather than fully describe or evaluate the program mentioned. Besides spotlighting the practicality of the lifecycle framework, these examples also reflect the foundation's intent, the first element in a capacity-building logic model.

Before showcasing these examples, let's look first at the concept of *capacity grantmaking.*

Capacity Grantmaking

Many foundations have engaged in "capacity building" grants for years through investments in management, infrastructure, buildings, or endowments. However, even those historically engaged would agree that the term "capacity building" has now come to represent a new field of practice, one that has elevated prior individual practices into something over and beyond what went before.

Today's capacity-building movement is an evolutionary cross between yesterday's *technical assistance* grants, made for specific "functional" improvements, and *evaluation,* which, in many circles, tended to measure *program* outcomes, rather than *organizational* measurements.

Foundations make *capacity grants* or establish *capacity initiatives* to boost the competency of nonprofit organizations in which they have some mission-related stake. Rather than making *program* grants that further nonprofit activities and services, *capacity* grants strengthen the overall functioning of the organization through strategic investments in management, staff, governance, finance, systems, marketing, planning, and other infrastructural requirements. For capacity grantmakers, these are usually not "either or" investments. In the best of circumstances, foundations make program grants *and* capacity grants to important community organizations compatible with their own missions.

Capacity grantmaking generally takes two forms:

- *Individual capacity grants* made to single grantees for specific and individuated capacity improvements, such as strategic plans, board training, development and marketing functions, audits or financial

> Foundations make capacity grants or establish capacity initiatives to boost the competency of nonprofit organizations in whom they have some mission-related stake. Rather than making program grants that further nonprofit activities and services, *capacity* grants strengthen the overall functioning of the organization through strategic investments in management, staff, governance, finance, systems, marketing, planning, and other infrastructural requirements.

system upgrades, or any number of other single capacity-building functions; and

- *Capacity programs or initiatives* designed to strengthen and improve the operating performance of a cluster of grantees. Capacity programs offer a customized but "wholesale" approach to strengthening nonprofit competence. The strength of capacity programs is their ability to improve performance, both individually and collectively. And though their methods may differ, their intent is the same: to strengthen a set of grantees in specific capacity areas that have been identified by either the grantees themselves or by the foundation.

The lifecycle approach is perfectly convertible to both single capacity grants and foundation-sponsored capacity-building activities.

Lifecycle Capacity Grants

Just as each programmatic field has patterns of performance, so too organizations develop in certain patterns or stages, each with its own set of typical characteristics and predictable challenges. Assessing a grantee's capacity starting point and setting stage-appropriate expectations for desired improvements becomes almost instinctive using lifecycle theory. Viewed through the lifecycle lens, funders can "zoom in" on required capacity improvements within the context of a particular developmental stage.

The *Nonprofit Lifecycle Reference Guide* presented in Chapter 4 details the typical lifecycle characteristics that nonprofits will experience at each developmental stage. These characteristics become funding opportunities for foundations interested in investing in nonprofit capacity. The *Nonprofit Lifecycle Reference Guide's* accompanying listing of *desired performance outcomes* will also help funders shape the expected outcome of their investments in a realistic way that is both stage- and performance-based.

For example, let's suppose that a grantee's lifecycle stage is the *growth stage* (the stage when nonprofits must increase their internal capacity to keep up with growing service demand). Referring to the *Nonprofit Lifecycles Reference Guide* it is determined that:

- Although the nonprofit has a number of good programs, their current "all things to all people" approach cannot be sustained.

- The board is made up of several excellent members who give their personal "all," but as a group, the board has not yet gelled or formalized its functioning.

As much sense as the lifecycles approach makes to foundations conceptually, grantees, too, find lifecycle dynamics intuitive and refreshingly respectful of "where they are."

118

- The organization is highly grant dependent, and seems to piece together funding rather than operate with a solid backbone of support and revenue.

- The business office is not able to produce financial reports helpful for analysis or decision-making.

There are several individual investment opportunities here, but the most comprehensive, and best place to start, is with funding a strategic or business planning process that helps the management and board:

- Focus in on a sustainable product mix, consistent with market need, their own distinctive competence, and sustainable financial requirements;

- Address the type of board composition and structure required to govern the organization effectively; and,

- Analyze staff composition needed to manage the various program and administrative functions.

Conversely, you could take one or another of these components and make a specific investment in one single capacity opportunity. One thing to remember, though, about the *growth stage.* Besides being the most expensive stage, it is also the most complex stage, making it nearly impossible to address one capacity element without it having a spin-off effect on other elements. So, in this example, it would be nearly impossible to fund the grant dependency area without looking at the product and program mix as well.

Many foundations currently use the lifecycles framework presented in this book in their own initial grant review, and encourage their grantees to use its concepts, too. As much sense as the lifecycles approach makes to these foundations conceptually, they report that grantees, too, find lifecycle dynamics intuitive and refreshingly respectful of "where they are." Indeed, as I've taught lifecycle theory to nonprofits through the years, the universal feedback is, *If I didn't know better, I'd think you were describing our organization specifically.*

Lifecycle Self-Assessments

As useful as the lifecycle approach is for foundations to diagnos of nonprofit capacity, it makes an equally valuable self-diagnostic tool for promoting self-awareness and an expectation of self-care for nonprofits as they think about their internal functioning. In the next chapter, I describe how important it is for nonprofit organizations to understand capacity

> The lifecycle approach provides both a diagnostic framework as well as a common language for grantees to establish their capacity starting points and present their opportunities for improvement.

and to make improvements on their own, if they are to "take." Indeed, one of the greatest risks of capacity grantmaking, especially those grants that are externally induced, is that grantees will see the capacity investment as just another opportunity to attract funding, rather than making a capacity change that lasts.

For this reason, many foundations have come to embrace *self-assessments,* sometimes facilitated by an outside consultant, to determine how grantees view their current set of organizational competencies and areas for improvement. In this way, the lifecycle approach provides both a diagnostic framework as well as a common language for grantees to establish their capacity starting points and present their opportunities for improvement. The non-judgmental quality of lifecycle diagnostics helps to disarm the otherwise "dirty linen" connotation that sometimes accompanies sharing organizational in capacities. The lifecycle approach presumes *every* stage has its developmental challenges, and that these challenges are a normal part of achieving competence at that stage.

The *High Bridge Community Life Center,* a community-based nonprofit in Bronx, New York, adopted the lifecycle framework as the basis for its annual program report to the Edna McConnell Clark Foundation.[xxiv] An excerpt from this report is reproduced on page 121, with permission from the organization.

The *Highbridge* example illustrates how well the lifecycles approach works as a self-diagnostic instrument for nonprofits to: 1) identify their lifecycle stage; 2) understand its attendant capacity-building requirements in a stage-based context; and 3) clearly acknowledge opportunities for improvement and investment.

Some foundations now track the lifecycle stages of their grantees, the type of capacity improvements most generally requested, the scope and nature of their capacity grants made, and the corresponding performance outcomes ensuing.

The *Nonprofit Lifecycles Reference Guide* (found at the end of Chapter 4), along with the accompanying *Nonprofit Lifecycles Capacity Placement* diagnostic, (Figure 5) provides both foundations and nonprofits with the diagnostic tools necessary to assess lifecycle placement, the capacity starting point, and desired performance outcomes.

THE HIGHBRIDGE COMMUNITY LIFE CENTER: A GROWTH-STAGE ORGANIZATION
(excerpt from annual report to the Edna McConnell Clark Foundation, used with permission)

Organizational History
The Idea Stage – By making door-to-door contact with families and businesses in 1978-79, Dominican Sisters Ann Lovett and Mary Moynihan assessed the need for services in Highbridge, and founded Highbridge Community Life Center.

The Start-up Stage – Incorporated in 1979 with only a shoestring budget, the first few years were marked by frequent chaos and crisis. Community needs overwhelmed available staff and programs. Funding was a constant worry. However, enthusiasm ran high and a board of directors was formed in 1980 for moral support and technical advice.

Where We are Today
The Growth Stage – In many ways HCLC is an organization best characterized as in the *growth-stage:* programs and services are in demand as the organization struggles to find the best mix; personnel policies, management structure, and program tracking and evaluation are in place. The current executive director has been at the helm for thirteen years and is committed to moving the agency from the *growth-stage* to *maturity.* The following chart is a self-analysis of the agency's organizational maturity based on reflections of staff, management, and outside evaluators.

COMPONENT	STAGE	EVIDENCE	BARRIERS TO GROWTH
Programs	Maturity	Outcome objectives. Performance- based contracts. Contractual accountability. Program results. Partner new programs with established ones. Secure sources of funding.	Space.
Management	Growth	Consistent policy implementation. Regular management meetings.	Unequal supervisor ratio. 65% of staff three years or less. Demand exceeds ability to supply service. Management fatigue.
Board of Directors	Growth	Moral support. Informal advice. Technical expertise. Financial support. Fiscal supervision.	Little hierarchy between board and staff. Demands of ownership need to be explored.
Financial resources	Growth	Safe sources of funds. Diversity. Quality accounting. Fiscal management. Performance-based contracts.	Delay in payment on contracts.
Administrative systems	Maturity	Job descriptions. Personnel policies. Employee handbook. Vacation records. Benefit package.Consistent salaries.	Managers need to take more responsibility for budget and spending.

Figure 5: Nonprofit Lifecycle Capacity Placement

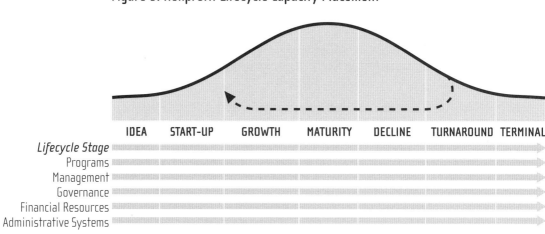

Investing in Capacity Initiatives

The *Nonprofit Lifecycle Capacity Placement* (Figure 5), although meant primarily as a self-assessment guide for nonprofits, also provides foundations with an excellent diagnostic tool to assess and invest in grantee capacity.

The lifecycles framework provides foundations with a solid intellectual basis for creating capacity initiatives and an equally practical investment tool as well.

Take for example Rose Community Foundation. In its first seven years (1995-2002), the foundation made several thousand grants in support of nonprofit organizations across the greater Denver community. While many of these grants met or exceeded expectations, the Foundation's senior program staff recognized a common challenge: project funding occasionally did not achieve the desired impact because some grantees lacked the infrastructure to adequately implement and sustain them.

Realizing that the Foundation's goals could best be achieved by strong grantees aligned with its strategic objectives, Rose's program staff began looking for a systemic way to strengthen selected grantees. They sought a model that could promote organizational development and encourage sound fiscal practices. Using the lifecycle approach to capacity outlined in this book, the Foundation's five senior program officers pooled just over $2 million from their respective grant budgets to fund a cross-program capacity initiative called "BOOST" ~ *Building Organizational Operating Strength Together.*

BOOST's first round launched with eight *growth-stage* grantees selected by foundation staff to participate in a three-year, intensive capacity-building program.

Like many successful capacity programs, BOOST was designed with five underlying precepts:

- Each grantee had an *established market for its services* and was providing programming important to the community.

- Grantees were *ready, willing, and able* to participate in an intensive framework.

- Selected grantees were facing a *critical juncture* and were willing to articulate this challenge in an open and honest manner at the outset of the acceptance process.

- Each organization would be represented by a *leadership team* consisting of at least two board members, the Executive Director and one other senior staff or board member.

- Grantees demonstrated an *openness to change* since, like any capacity program, BOOST was all about capacity improvement, which generally results in organizational change.

The Foundation's 2008 final report on the BOOST initiative notes that the direct and indirect results of BOOST exceeded all expectations for the program's eight grantees, their consultants, and the Foundation itself. An evaluation conducted by Denver-based Corona Research notes that "the lifecycles approach validated the experiences and challenges of the grantees, and assisted the consultants in working with the organizations 'where they were' in their development. The model was a critical component for organizational self-assessment and provided a framework for thinking about stage-appropriate capacity while helping to depersonalize barriers and problems." [xxv]

Another example of a stage-specific capacity program is ArtsLAB, a collaborative capacity program sponsored by the Minnesota-based Bush, Jerome and Saint Paul Foundations. My colleagues and I designed this program following a study the Bush Foundation conducted of small and mid-sized Minnesota arts organizations. Among several findings, the study revealed that the average budget of these groups (in the late 1990s) was $200,000 and the average age twenty years. The study further described participants' perceptions that many arts groups become "stuck" around the $200,000 - $250,000 budget range. So collaboratively, the three sponsoring foundations created ArtsLAB, a capacity program to strengthen small and mid-sized neighborhood-based arts groups. Designed as a sin-

The lifecycles approach validated the experiences and challenges of the grantees, and assisted the consultants in working with the organizations 'where they were' in their development. The model was a critical component for organizational self-assessment and provided a framework for thinking about stage-appropriate capacity while helping to depersonalize barriers and problems.

gle-stage capacity program, ArtsLAB facilitated participants thinking about their own organizational dynamics and the optimal operational structure that best suited their mission. [xxvi]

ArtsLAB and the first round of BOOST represent *stage-specific* capacity programs. Each program was specifically designed to address capacity issues common in the *start-up stage* (ArtsLAB) and the *growth-stage* (BOOST).

Indeed, foundations get the most bang for their buck when they gear capacity programs to either the *start-up* or *growth stages*. These are the stages where nonprofits are becoming operational for the first time, as in the case of *start-ups*, or need to build more muscular "capacity legs" to accommodate increased service demand in the *growth stage*.

More often than not though, when foundations invest in capacity programs, they by necessity need to select grantees that fall in various lifecycle stages ~ and this is where the lifecycles approach to capacity really shines. Rather than setting one-sized capacity expectations with boilerplate supports, the lifecycle approach meets each grantee where they are, and honoring that starting place, develops supports that will strengthen their capacity.

In 2007, when the Gifford Foundation in Syracuse, New York made the decision to move from a competitive grant-making approach to one that incorporated capacity building for its nonprofit grantees and community partners, the foundation chose the lifecycles capacity model as its organizing framework for both capacity assessment and investment.

Among a host of initiatives, the foundation created ADVANS ~ *Advancing and Developing the Value and Assets of Nonprofits in Syracuse*. The first round of ADVANS brought together nine organizations from varying lifecycle stages ranging from *start-up* to *turnaround*. The Foundation handselected each grantee because of the importance of their mission to the greater Syracuse community. However, by virtue of their different lifecycle stages, the capacity requirements and readiness levels of these nine groups were quite dissimilar. Consequently, the Foundation's capacity investments and program supports differed too.

Grantees in *growth* and *maturity* undertook a three-year program facilitated by local consultants trained in the lifecycle model. The consultants led each group through a lifecycle capacity assessment and a business planning process, with Gifford committing $120,000 over three years towards each group's business plan implementation.

Grantees in *start-up*, *turnaround* and *decline* also undertook a lifecycle assessment under the guidance of a trained lifecycles consultant. Once completed, these grantees identified infrastructure areas that would bene-fit from the Foundation's one-time $25,000 investment.

Early in the process, an executive from one ADVANS organization summarized her experience with the program in this way: "I've been with our organization since it began. The ADVANS process made me realize that there is capacity no matter what your level. The honesty of the pro-cess was liberating. I was scared at first, but the lifecycle assessment gave me a safe place to figure out where we are and embrace our capacity no mat-ter what stage we're in."

This concept of "safe space" is one of the most real benefits of the life-cycle self-assessment and approach. The non-judgmental, diagnostic nature of the assessment instrument and process encourages grantees to be open and honest. Most important, the process promotes *self-awareness* and an expectation of *self-care* as grantees realize, often for the first time, that capacity is their responsibility. The following chapter, *Internalizing Capacity,* continues this discussion of the importance of self-awareness as nonprofits take what they learn in capacity initiatives to heart.

This chapter spotlighted three local capacity programs among a host of other national and local foundations that over the past decades have adopt-ed the lifecycles framework as the basis for their capacity initiatives. The mechanics and results of two long-term lifecycle-based, national capacity programs have been documented by the Ford Foundation in the booklet *Investing in Capacity: How the Working Capital Program Promotes Sustainable Change;* and by the Andy Warhol Foundation in its 2005 Report *The Warhol Initiative: Capacity Building in the Visual Arts.* These reports are well worth the read.

Whether employed by national, local, or regional foundations, the life-cycle approach gives foundations and their nonprofit partners a common language and similar conceptual framework from which to think about and discuss operating capacity. Best yet, with more than two decades in practice, the lifecycles model is a proven capacity tool that makes sound practical and financial sense to both foundation investors and their non-profit beneficiaries.

> This concept of "safe space" is one of the most real benefits of the lifecycle self-assessment and approach. The non-judg-mental, diagnostic nature of the assessment instrument and process encourages grantees to be open and honest.

11

INTERNALIZING CAPACITY

When patterns are broken new worlds can emerge.

Tuli Kupferberg

Whether lifecycle based or not, the explicit goal of capacity-building programs is to strengthen nonprofits' organizational competence and performance. But capacity programs generally have something else in common, too. They are also about organizational *change*. Granted, the degree of change required may vary from program to program, and from grantee to grantee. But by their very nature, capacity programs seek to induce a better method of performance ~ and that generally means a series of at least small internal changes, and more likely, a larger set of changes in both the organization's actions and, possibly, its thought patterns.

The first ten chapters of this book have established the rationale for a lifecycles approach to managing and funding nonprofit capacity. But, in addition to its lifecycle aspect, capacity is actually *an internal dynamic,* something that funders, consultants, and other external parties must continually keep in mind as we seek to "build" capacity from the outside.

Neither capacity nor change comes without cost. And though foundation support is essential to strengthening nonprofit capabilities, we must not forget the *internal costs* nonprofits pay to undertake the type of organizational change some capacity programs require.

This chapter takes a deeper look at the internal change dynamics that generally accompany intensive capacity-building activities. Many of the four dynamics discussed apply to individual capacity grants that have a long-term intent, such as strategic planning, board development, or financial restructuring. But even more so, these concepts describe the behavioral dynamics and mindset shifts that accompany successful multi-year, foundation-sponsored capacity programs.

Just as the lifecycle diagnostics presented earlier in this book are meant to provide a deeper understanding of the developmental characteristics of nonprofit capacity, this chapter explores the types of thought processes and behavior shifts that generally accompany change-based capacity initiatives.

This chapter tackles the hand-in-glove relationship of *capacity building* and *organizational change.* Indeed, I have always found it curious that capacity initiatives don't advertise themselves as "change" programs. One of the most profound moments in any consulting engagement or foundation-sponsored capacity program is when participants realize that the consultancy or capacity grant will require them to change their longstanding practices. *I didn't know how much we would have to change!*

Yet, since few of us, organizationally or personally, walk willingly down the path of change, maybe it's better that capacity programs aren't explicit about their change angle. We all like the familiar, and those involved in capacity initiatives are no exception.

So this chapter focuses attention on the internal dynamics of capacity-building in a way meant to complement lifecycle theory, but provides no illusion about the depth of change that some organizations undergo as a result of capacity-building activities. The lessons presented, although not everyday philanthropic concepts are, nonetheless, well-grounded in theories of organizational and personal change. They also reflect my thirty years as an organizational consultant, and another dozen or so years as a family counselor helping individuals and organizations strengthen their capabilities and competencies to achieve their personal and organizational goals.

And so I present four of the dynamics necessary for internal change ~ *internalizing insights and learnings, identifying the organization's mindset, reframing the mindset,* and *creating new habits* ~ to both elucidate the relationship between effective capacity building and sustainable organizational change, and to honor the profound changes nonprofits embrace every day in search of organizational capacity.

Figure 11: Four Dynamics of Organizational Change

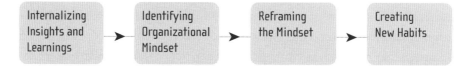

| Internalizing Insights and Learnings | → | Identifying Organizational Mindset | → | Reframing the Mindset | → | Creating New Habits |

Internalizing Insights and Learnings

The ability to *internalize* program insights and learning is among the most important processes that must occur for capacity efforts of any kind to be effective. In the vernacular, internalization is the "getting it" factor.

Fundamental as it may seem, a nonprofit's ability to understand *why* capacity and performance are needed is critical to its organizational success. I've learned through the years not to take an organization's ability to internalize program learnings for granted. Indeed, as early as possible in the capacity engagement, it is important to determine participants' likelihood to internalize the changes inherent in the program's methods, and to make the program and its supports "theirs," rather than the funder's or consultant's.

Nonprofits' traditional reliance on foundations and other donors for their financial well-being can make this easier said than done. Indeed, alleviating the *dependency factor* is some foundation's first reason for adopting a capacity approach to grantmaking. Yet, the question of dependency is a tricky one since so many nonprofits "depend on" and require annual subsidies to fund their operating budgets. For example, studies show that in the arts, contributions from foundations and other donors represent 40 percent or more of annual income. It's no wonder nonprofits become psychologically as well as financially dependent on outside funders for their well-being!

But leaving systemic dependencies aside for a moment, we can otherwise predict a grantee's ability to internalize capacity initiatives by understanding what personality psychologists call their *locus of control*.

Locus of control is a clinical term, adopted by organizational behaviorists, to describe *how organizations think about who is in charge of their lives*. Organizations with an *internal* locus of control feel responsible for and in charge of their own destiny. They view their organizational well-being, performance, and results as self-dependent and not caused by outside factors. They see a strong relationship between their own actions and what happens around them. They perceive themselves as independent achievers, and approach the world in this way. This does not mean that they act without influence. Rather, when faced with change, opportunity, or need for adaptation, no matter what pain it may entail, they feel compelled to rise to it, steeped in security about a generally positive outcome, and having turned the need for change into their own idea.

Organizations with an internal locus of control are "dream team" participants for capacity programs. They come into the program with an understanding of what the program (or capacity grant) can do for them. They have a fairly accurate self-assessment of their starting point, and a clear expectation of how they will use the program's technical supports

Locus of control is a clinical term that describes how organizations think about who is in charge of their lives. Organizations with an *internal* locus of control feel responsible for and in charge of their own destiny. Organizations with an *external* locus of control operate from a belief that others, outside themselves, control their destiny.

and resources to further their already self-defined journey toward higher performance and overall effectiveness. Capacity grants or programs aimed at nonprofits that are self-dependent will generally solidify their results quite quickly. These are supportive investments in nonprofits already in tune with their lifecycle stage and where they need to go from here.

Nonprofits with an *external* locus of control are another story. These groups operate from a belief that someone else controls their destiny ~ and that someone is generally an outside funder.

Externally-dependent nonprofits are often insecure and unsure about what it will take to influence their future. Many also operate out of unconscious thought patterns that may have quit working for them years earlier but now form their *default mindset.* [xxvii]

I am reminded of a vivid example of externally-dependent nonprofit thinking. Several years ago my colleagues and I designed a study for The Minneapolis Foundation on the *Financial Health of Minnesota's Nonprofits.* In addition to collecting longitudinal financial data about Minnesota's nonprofits, it was also meant to capture nonprofits' perceptions and current or changing attitudes about a variety of financial topics. [xxviii]

One of the survey questions asked, *Who is most responsible for the financial success or failure of your organization?* Respondents had four possible answers: a) board of directors, b) executive director, c) development/finance director, and d) other.

Every survey year, without fail, several nonprofits checked the "other" category. This is a classic example of external locus of control in action.

The key challenge for any capacity program is to help *externally-dependent* participants, those who feel their well-being is outside their own control, to become *internally-dependent,* self-determined organizations. This is what it means to *internalize* a program, and indeed, it is the only way a capacity program's lessons and methods will have enduring impact.

Sometimes this is simply a matter of education. Hard as it may be to imagine, there are still nonprofits that don't know they are in charge of their own well-being. Some understand it on one level, but have not stopped recently to examine the incongruities between their thought patterns and behavioral practices. These are the groups that have spent so much time on bended knee that they may now live out a pattern of unconscious, unhealthy funder dependency.

Classic psychologists would argue that anyone needing to be told they're in charge of their own destiny is a far-cry away from having an internal locus of control. But my experience proves otherwise. With the right capacity investment (generally in management or board develop-

Organizations with an internal locus of control are "dream team" participants for capacity programs. They come into the program with an understanding of what the program can do for them, a fairly accurate self-assessment of their starting point, and a clear expectation of how they will use the program's technical supports and resources to further their already self-defined journey toward higher performance and overall effectiveness.

ment), many nonprofits can get to a self-defining mindset faster than one might imagine.

There are innumerable examples where programmatically sophisticated nonprofits operate on inaccurate information. They (and their board members, in particular) mistakenly think that to be "nonprofit" they can't have surpluses, or that foundations won't give them money if they don't run occasional operating deficits. (Promise me, funders, that this isn't true.)

When a foundation-sponsored capacity program tells these otherwise smart groups that their "facts" are incorrect, many can make the necessary course corrections on their own steam. There is no substitute for solid information, delivered through training programs, capacity grants, or capacity initiatives.

Encouraging internally-motivated nonprofits to adopt new capacity behavior patterns is generally just a matter of pointing them in the right direction. But for those more externally-dependent, we need to take a deeper look into their organizational thought processes, or *mindset.*

Identifying the Organization's Mindset

"Mindset" is how we think. It is simultaneously a cognitive and emotional process, a system of conscious, logical thought patterns mixed with unconscious and sometimes illogical thoughts, working together in a self-fulfilling manner. Transforming externally-dependent organizations into self-directed entities starts with an examination of the organization's prevailing *mindset,* the internal messages that form the organization's collective mentality and consequently shape its performance and behavior.[xxix]

Organizational mindsets don't stray far from their key individuals. How individuals within the organization think, so does the organization. Organizational mindsets frequently function on "auto-pilot." Once programmed, they go through the motions without conscious regard to their effects. Many organizational psychologists believe that to change behavior, personally or collectively, we must first understand the auto-pilot quality of the default mindset.[xxx]

Understanding an organization's mindset requires first listening for the *subtext* of what's being said. Sometimes what an organization says is very different than how it thinks and behaves. This is particularly true in competitive capacity grantmaking situations, where a proposal is required to gain a grant award or to enter the program. Too frequently a development officer writes the proposal, beautifully linking the organization's needs with the program's intents and mechanisms. Once accepted or interviewed for the program, though, it becomes obvious that the proposal's words are out

> Organizational mindsets frequently function on "auto-pilot." Once programmed, they go through the motions without conscious regard to their effects.

of sync with organizational mindset and historical performance.

Foundations and consultants involved in capacity-building programs should always be listening on three levels: *the text level* (what's being said); *the hyper-text level* (do the needs of the organization match the intent of the initiatives?); and *the sub-text level* (does the organization understand how much it will have to change to take advantage of the programs mechanisms?). It's in the *sub-text* that the prevailing mindset is revealed.

Some would argue that instituting a set of behavioral practices ~ regular submission of financial statements, requirements that organizations "operate in the black," attendance at program-sponsored seminars, or mandatory board development ~ brings about capacity. And indeed, these things do substantially improve capacity in internally-driven organizations. But for capacity programs to "take" in externally-dependent organizations, their prevailing thought patterns may need to be re-visited and possibly re-framed.

As you read through the following re-framing steps keep in mind how much easier it is to grasp these facts intellectually, then it is for a nonprofit (or anyone, for that matter) to actually incorporate them into practice.

Re-framing the Organizational Mindset

There are at least two critical ingredients to the re-framing process.

- *Understanding the purpose the mindset serves within the context of an organization's reality.*[xxxi] This purpose usually has self-preservational characteristics, originally set in motion by some legitimate behavior once necessary to the organization's self-interest but now counterproductive to it. The key to reversing an externally-dependent mindset lies in helping the organization to examine and "own" its mindset, and then to see how these unconscious messages, in fact, limit the future. Don't expect this realization to come in one "big bang." It often takes multiple times planting the right questions, with the right people, before the re-framing process begins to occur.

- *Visualizing what capacity might look like if the nonprofit was organizationally healthy and believed it could effect positive changes in its future.* What would it be like to be well-managed, appropriately governed and staffed, and financially healthy? What would it take to get there? Capacity programs that have strategic planning components can be helpful here in visualizing higher performance.

These re-framing tips bring up the question of *readiness,* which is a frequent concern especially in multiple-year capacity initiatives. Easy as it would be to accept only the "ready" into capacity programs, readiness may not occur for some groups until a year or two into the program. But whether ready or not at the outset, the sooner capacity programs can catch (or induce) organizations in their re-framing process, the more likely that change is to be sustainable. Re-framing that happens near or after the program's conclusion lacks the benefit of the reinforcing supports which are a fundamental part of most capacity initiatives.

> Habit change means repeating positive, self-actualizing behaviors over and again, until they become ingrained in the mindset and part of the behavioral repertoire, even when no one is looking.

Creating New Habits

A long-running debate in the psychology field has been whether mindset change *must* precede behavioral changes or if, through the process of consistently reinforcing behavioral change, a person's thought patterns will naturally follow. In other words, do people have to "get it" before they can "do it"? Behaviorists believe that if you reinforce certain conscious or unconscious behaviors long enough, mindset will automatically follow. The day will come when, with enough longitudinal experience under our belts, capacity-grantmakers and consultants will also begin to engage in this same type of debate.

Today, organizational behaviorists emphasize the importance of *habit change,* rather than singular behavior changes, as the key predictor of sustainable personal and organizational change. Habits are behavior patterns developed through frequent repetition.

One of the most approachable works in this regard comes from John D. Adams' research on the *six dimensions of sustainable habit change,* included here with the author's permission.

Six Dimensions of Sustainable Habit Change

1. A heartfelt commitment to succeeding that includes the belief that change is possible and desirable

2. Sufficient dissatisfaction with the current state

3. A clear goal, vision, or outcome plus a practical first action step or two

4. Mechanisms or structures that require regular repetitions of the newly adopted habit

5. A willingness to be patient and to trust the process

6. Some kind of outer or inner "wake-up call" that focuses awareness on the limits or inappropriateness of the current state [xxxii]

Tough as it is to analyze and own one's default mindset and then dislodge and reframe it, changing behavior and habits is that much harder and then some. Think about this personally. How many times have you tried to quit some bad habit? You know in your head that it's bad for you, but all the cognitive understanding in the world does not necessarily result in the ability to stop smoking, overeating, biting our nails, etc.

It reminds me of a definition of maturity I once read. *Maturity is doing what you should, even when no one's looking.* Likewise, habit change means repeating positive, self-actualizing behaviors over and again, until they become ingrained in the mindset and part of the behavioral repertoire, even when no one is looking.

It is common and, in fact, usual for organizations to slip a time or two on the path to habit change and increased capacity. These slips, whether unconscious missteps into old behavior or conscious temporary disengagement, are a normal and predictable part of the change process. Old habits die hard, and effective change will create confusion and sometimes a temporary sense of disorientation as old behaviors and thought processes are discarded in favor of the new. Multiple-year capacity initiatives give organizations the time and breathing room within which to try on new behaviors, to practice and modify them, and to get ready to figure out how to sustain them at the program's close.

Since organizational habits are rooted in the mindsets and behaviors of people, I can't close this chapter without focusing on the central role of the change agent, or, in one author's terms, the path-maker[xxxiii] in creating habit change. The path-maker's role is one of confident persuasion, engaging others to see the promise of the future from the reality of the present, and providing a practical and frequently inspirational map to get from one destination to the other.

But sustainable capacity-related change and internalization cannot rest on the shoulders of one person alone. In the *turnaround* stage, we speak glowingly about the change agent, a heroic type who often single handedly reverses the fortune of a nonprofit or commercial entity.

In capacity programs, change is even more complex, requiring multiple stakeholders to weave together a support team for the change they have mutually agreed upon. This is frequently why capacity initiatives build *peer support* and *multiple-person team participation* into their support structures. The value of the peer approach is that no matter how ready

Multiple-year capacity initiatives give organizations the time and breathing room within which to try on new behaviors, to practice and modify them, and to get ready to figure out how to sustain them at the program's close.

participants are when they enter the program, they have the benefit of watching each other adapt thinking and behavior over time. As one capacity program participant put it, *If so-and-so can change, I guess I can too. He's even more stuck in his ways than I am.*

The other reason capacity-related change and internalization is different than the turnaround mindset has to do with the word "crisis." Creating sustainable change is much harder than facing a crisis. It is an internal acknowledgement that things need to be different, and a collective and public commitment to making it so. This takes the efforts of the whole organization, not the single-handed workings of one heroic superstar.

So these four factors form the internal and behavioral dynamics that must accompany sustainable organizational change: *internalizing insights and learnings, understanding and re-framing the organizational mindset,* and *creating new habits.* Singly and together, these dynamics work to ensure that change-based capacity grants or programs will improve nonprofits' *self-awareness* along with their *competencies,* and in that way provide lasting value for their organizations, constituencies, and communities.

FINAL THOUGHTS

In closing, I offer this *capacity credo*, a set of five beliefs that have framed the basis of my consulting practice over the past twenty years and have helped to shape the contents of this book as well.

Capacity Credo
- *Capacity counts.* Without organizational competence, nonprofits cannot achieve or sustain long-term program delivery or mission success.

- *Capacity costs.* Whether through self-investments of nonprofit time, resources, and energy, or through capacity-building grants from outside funders, investments in nonprofit capacity don't come cheap. All the more reason to invest as strategically and wisely as possible.

- *Capacity is not a one-size-fits-all phenomenon.* Rather, nonprofit capacity will look and be defined differently depending on an organization's lifecycle stage. High performing behavior at one stage may, in fact, be underachievement at another.

- *Capacity is the first step toward organizational performance and effectiveness.* Capacity anchors nonprofit performance. Without it, nonprofits can't hope to achieve high performance or make a long-term impact on society's well-being.

- *Capacity, even when externally supported, is still an internal dynamic.* Thus, even *lifecycle* capacity-building investments must still be internalized by the supported organization if they are to become sustainable over the long haul.

The real work of the nonprofit sector happens within the context of mission, market, and program ~ the daily delivery of services to those who need them. Yet, that work is both facilitated and strengthened when supported by a strong platform of organizational capacity.

The centerpiece of this book is lifecycle theory. It is an approach to strengthening nonprofit capacity that is grounded in developmental and economic theory, and provides an eminently practical tool to capture the stage-related tasks and challenges that accompany each phase of nonprofit development.

Lifecycle dynamics are an everyday reality for all organizations, non-profit or otherwise, in all stages of life. Nonprofits instinctively know this and thus resonate immediately to lifecycle diagnostics as a way to understand and articulate their growing pains and to confront the accompanying challenges. That's why the lifecycle approach to capacity works so well. It takes a holistic approach to capacity, one that recognizes the importance of mission and programs, but values, too, the entire organization as a delivery mechanism.

As the call for nonprofit services becomes even greater and foundation funding in ever-increasing demand, lifecycle recognition ensures both nonprofits and grantmakers that their valuable investments of time, money, and effort will indeed hit the capacity mark.

Although more than a century in the making, lifecycle theory provides a new organizational language and framework for nonprofits and grantmakers to think and talk about organizational competencies and their corollary expectations. A nonprofit theater client described it this way: *When I am producing a show, I understand my artistic "walls" ~ the boundaries within which the show needs to stay to be successful. But when it comes to my organization, I never knew where the walls were until we had bounced in and out of bounds so many times my head was spinning. The lifecycle stages have become our organizational walls.*

And so this book ends as it began, firm in the contention that, if society does indeed depend on nonprofit organizations for essential service delivery, then these organizations must have the wherewithal to become strong, capable, and durable institutions.

Lifecycle diagnostics has helped me shape, what others have called, a hands-on, but wisdom-based practice. I offer it now to you, nonprofits and foundations, academics and consultants, in our mutual and timeless quest to strengthen the capacity of those nonprofits in whom we are all heavily invested, as they continue to build strong, healthy communities for those that need them the most.

REFERENCES

[i] Reprinted with permission from the Urban Institute *Press*.

[ii] *Nonprofit Almanac.* Independent Sector. 2001.

[iii] Foundation Center *2000 Giving Patterns.* New York.

[iv] Numerous studies of organizational effectiveness support the lifecycle approach to effectiveness, the works of Cameron and Whetton (1981), and Quinn and Cameron (1983) in particular.

[v] Stevens, Susan Kenny. "Making Working Capital Work." *Foundation News and Commentary.* July/August, 2000.

[vi] Kramer, M. "Helping to Prevent a Culture of Inadequacy." *Chronicle on Philanthropy.* April, 2000.

[vii] Letts, C.; Ryan, W.; Grossman A. *High Performance Nonprofits: Managing Upstream for Greater Impact.* Wiley. New York. 1998.

[viii] Backer, Thomas. "Strengthening Nonprofits: Foundation Initiatives for Nonprofit Organizations." *Building Capacity in Nonprofit Organizations.* The Urban Institute. Washington DC. 2001.

[ix] Reprinted with permission of the Marino Institute

[x] The *normative crisis model* focuses on the importance of impulses to developmental change. All normative crisis models work from the assumption that it is an *internally motivated crisis,* or in organizational behavior terms, *critical juncture* that sparks movement to another developmental stage.

[xi] Gibb, A.A.; Dyson, J. "Stimulating the Growth of Owner Managed Firms." *Success and Failure in Small Business.* Gower Publishing. Aldershot, England. 1984.

[xii] S. H. Hanks (1990) in his doctoral research study coined the phrase *disengagement stages* to refer to organizations that had "capped" their growth for one of two reasons: *life-style disengagement* in which owners had made a conscious choice to keep their firms small; or *capped growth disengagements,* generally older, less complex organizations, that had disengaged from growth after successfully expanding to what they perceived as an optimum, albeit modest size. See Hanks, S.H.

An Empirical Examination of the Organizational Lifecycle in High Technology Organizations. Doctor of Philosophy Dissertation, University of Utah. Salt Lake City. UT. 1990.

xiii   See *Harvard Business Review* (1972 and 1998) for a full text of Greiner's lifecycle business theory.

xiv   Hanks, 1990.

xv   Greiner, Larry E., "Evolution and Revolution as Organizations Grow." *Harvard Business Review.* May-June, 1998.

xvi   Adizes, Ichak. *Corporate Lifecycles: How and Why Corporations Grow, Die and What to Do About It.* Prentice Hall. Englewood Cliffs NJ. 1988.

xvii   Stevens, Susan Kenny. "Helping Founders Succeed." *Grantmakers in the Arts Reader.* Autumn, 1999.

xviii   Harrison and Shirom in their book *Organizational Diagnosis and Assessment* (Thousand Oaks CA. 1999) devote an entire chapter to organizational lifecycles and list four ways in which the lifecycle approach contributes to a practitioner's understanding of organizational diagnostics.

xix   Reprinted with permission of Sage Publishing.

xx   *Income-based spending* refers to a practice of spending according to actual, rather than budgeted, income. It correlates to *income-based budgeting,* a practice of starting the budgeting process with realistic income projections and setting expenses accordingly. See *All the Way to the Bank.* Stevens, Susan Kenny and Anderson, Lisa M. The Stevens Group. St. Paul MN. 1997.

xxi   Portions of this chapter were excerpted from my previous article "Helping Founders Succeed," published originally in the *Grantmakers in the Arts Reader,* Autumn, 1999, and subsequently adapted in LarsonAllen's *EFFECT Magazine,* Winter, 2002.

xxii   These 12 principles are excerpted from my doctoral research dissertation *In Their Own Words: The Entrepreneurial Behavior of Nonprofit Founders.* Doctor of Philosophy Dissertation, Union Institute, Cincinnati, OH., 2003.

xxiii   Tierney, Thomas J., *The Nonprofit Sector's Leadership Deficit.* The Bridgespan Group, March 2006.

xxiv This excerpt is used with the permission of *Highbridge Community Life Center* with special thanks to Brother Ed Phelen F.S.C., its author and executive director, and to the Edna McConnell Clark Foundation's Sue Bellinger for bringing this example to my attention.

xxv From *BOOST, A Report of Rose Community Foundation's Three-Year Capacity Building Initiative*. Denver CO. 2008. Available from the Foundation at rcfdenver.org/publications_reports.htm. This report also cites the action learning assessment produced by Corona Research Inc., of Denver CO. July 2007.

xxvi From *ArtsLAB* Program Description available from www.larsonallen.com/publicservice

xxvii Adams, John D. "Six Dimensions of a Sustainable Consciousness." *Perspectives on Business and Global Change*. World Business Academy. Vol. 14; no. 2. 2000.

xxviii This study, and variations, was also administered in Illinois, under sponsorship of the Illinois Facilities Fund and the Chicago Donors Forum, and in Alberta, Canada by the Kahanoff Foundation.

xxix Adams, 2000.

xxx Adams, 2000.

xxxi Kets De Vries, Manfred F.R. and Balazs, Katherina. "Transforming the Mindset of the Organization." *Administration and Society*. Beverly Hills, CA. January, 1999.

xxxii Adams, 2000.

xxxiii Robbins, Harvey; Finley, Michael. *Why Change Doesn't Work*. Harper and Row. New York. 1996.

BIBLIOGRAPHY

Adams, John D. "Six Dimensions of a Sustainable Consciousness." *Perspectives on Business and Global Change.* World Business Academy. Vol. 14; no. 2. 2000.

Adizes, Ichak. *Corporate Lifecycles: How and Why Corporations Grow, Die and What to Do About It.* Prentice Hall. Englewood Cliffs NJ. 1988.

Backer, Thomas. "Strengthening Nonprofits: Foundation Initiatives for Nonprofit Organizations." *Building Capacity in Nonprofit Organizations.* The Urban Institute. Washington DC. 2001.

DeVita, Carol J. and Fleming, Cory; editors. *Building Capacity in Nonprofit Organizations.* The Urban Institute. Washington DC. 2001.

Dyer, W. Gibb, Jr. and Handler, Wendy. "Entrepreneurship and Family Business: Exploring the Connections." *Entrepreneurship, Theory and Practice,* Fall 1994.

Erikson, E.H. *The Life-cycle Completed, a Review.* Norton. New York. 1982.

Gibb, A.A. and Dyson, J. "Stimulating the Growth of Owner Managed Firms." *Success and Failure in Small Business.* Gower Publishing. Aldershot, England. 1984.

Greiner, Larry E., "Evolution and Revolution as Organizations Grow." *Harvard Business Review.* May-June, 1998.

Hanks, S.H. *An Empirical Examination of the Organizational Lifecycle in High Technology Organizations.* Doctor of Philosophy Dissertation, University of Utah. Salt Lake City, UT. 1990.

Harrison, Michael and Shirom, Arie. *Organizational Diagnosis and Assessment.* Sage. Thousand Oaks, CA. 1999.

Kets De Vries, Manfred F.R. and Balazs, Katherina. "Transforming the Mindset of the Organization." *Administration and Society.* Beverly Hills. January, 1999.

Kramer, M. "Helping to Prevent a Culture of Inadequacy." *Chronicle on Philanthropy.* April, 2000.

Letts, C.; Ryan, W.; Grossman A. *High Performance Nonprofits: Managing Upstream for Greater Impact.* Wiley. New York. 1998.

Lewin, K. *Field Theory in Social Science.* Harper and Row. New York. 1951.

Meyer, M. and Zucker, L. *Permanently Failing Organizations.* Sage. Newbury CA. 1989.

Osborne, Richard L., "Entrepreneurial Renewal." *Business Horizons.* November–December, 1992.

Quinn, R.E. and Cameron, K.S. "Lifecycles and Shifting Criteria on Effectiveness." *Management Science.* 1983.

Reik, T. *Listening with the Third Ear: The Inner Experience of a Psychoanalyst.* International Universities Press. New York. 1951.

Robbins, Harvey and Finley, Michael. *Why Change Doesn't Work.* Harper and Row. New York. 1996.

Rose Community Foundation. *BOOST: A Report of Rose Community Foundation's Three-year Capacity-Building Initiative.* Denver CO. 2008.

Rubenson, George C. and Gupta, Anil K. "Replacing the Founder: Exploding the Myth of Entrepreneur's Disease." *Business Horizons.* November–December, 1992.

Stein, Murray. *In Midlife: A Jungian Perspective.* Spring Publications. New York. 1983.

Stevens, Susan Kenny. "Alone Again, Naturally." A Working Capital Fund Case Study. University of San Francisco. 1999.

Stevens, Susan Kenny. *Growing Up Nonprofit™: The Seven Stages of Nonprofit Lifecycle Development.* The Stevens Group. St. Paul MN. 1988, 1990, 1993.

Stevens, Susan Kenny. "Helping Founders Succeed." *Grantmakers in the Arts Reader.* Autumn, 1999.

Stevens, Susan Kenny. *In Their Own Words: The Entrepreneurial Behavior of Nonprofit Founders.* Doctor of Philosophy Dissertation. Union Institute, Cincinnati, OH. 2003.

Stevens, Susan Kenny. "Making Working Capital Work." *Foundation News and Commentary.* July-August, 2000.

Stevens, Susan Kenny and Anderson, Lisa M. *All the Way to the Bank: Smart Money Management for Tomorrow's Nonprofit.* The Stevens Group. St. Paul MN. 1997.

Stevens, Susan Kenny and Espaldon, Diane. *Investing in Capacity: How the Working Capital Fund Promotes Sustainable Change.* Community Loan Technologies. Minneapolis MN. 2001.

The Stevens Group. *The Financial Health of Minnesota's Nonprofits.* The Minneapolis Foundation/Community Loan Technologies. Minneapolis MN. 1990, 1994, 1999.

Tierney, Thomas J., *The Nonprofit Sector's Leadership Deficit.* The Bridgespan Group. Boston, MA. March 2006.

Venture Philanthropy Partners. *Effective Capacity Building in Nonprofit Organizations.* Morino Institute. Reston VA. 2001.

Whetton, D. *Organizational Growth and Decline Processes.* Annual Review of Sociology. 1987.

INDEX

ABOUT THE AUTHOR

Susan Kenny Stevens is a nationally recognized consultant, author and lecturer on management, financial and organizational issues pertaining to philanthropy and the nonprofit sector. Her books and case studies are used nationally and internationally in university-based nonprofit management courses.

Dr. Stevens holds a Ph.D. in Organizational Behavior. Her doctoral research focused on the entrepreneurial behavior of nonprofit founders.

She and her husband Pat, the parents of two grown sons, make their home in Saint Paul, MN.

Order Nonprofit Lifecycles on line at
www.stagewiseenterprises.com or on Amazon.com.